Editor
Eric Migliaccio

Editor in Chief
Ina Massler Levin, M.A.

Creative Director
Karen J. Goldfluss, M.S. Ed.

Cover Artist
Diem Pascarella

Art Coordinator
Renée Mc Elwee

Imaging
James Edward Grace

Publisher

Mary D. Smith, M.S. Ed.

Author

Ruth Foster, M.Ed.

Teacher Created Resources
6421 Industry Way
Westminster, CA 92683
www.teachercreated.com

ISBN: 978-1-4206-3520-1

© 2013 Teacher Created Resources
Made in U.S.A.

Table of Contents

Introduction

How to Use This Book — Questions and Writing Practice — Vocabulary — Internet Usage — Internet Safety — Research Notes for Students

Introduction

We live in a world where the majority of research is now done on the internet. It is vital that we prepare our students by teaching them how to access this medium, think critically about the information gathered, and then demonstrate their mastery in both standardized-test and written-exam format.

21ˢᵗ Century Fact Finds: Using Online Research Tools to Reinforce Common Core Skills is a resource that does all of this and more. It hones such traditional educational skills as reading comprehension, critical thinking, and vocabulary building, while harnessing the modern power of the information-rich internet for classroom use.* This book allows students to thoughtfully and responsibly conduct research and learn on their own terms. Ultimately, this gives students a sense of ownership and a stake in learning.

*Note: All of the research tasks in this book can be completed using traditional sources (e.g., dictionaries, atlases, encyclopedias, etc.) if by necessity or preference.

How to Use This Book

This book consists of 25 stories. Each story is written at grade level with a word count of 425–550 words. Story topics are high-interest and written to hook a student's attention. For example, topics include a man who fell faster than sound, a hospital where there is no light, and floors purposefully built to squeak.

While each story is based on truth, there are varying degrees of factual inaccuracy. For example, a country may be in an incorrect location, a mammal may be called a reptile, or a historical event may be placed in the wrong century. Some stories have zero errors, while others have one, two, three, or even four errors.

No matter the number of errors, students are directed (by icons and words) to research specific topics using these tools:

- ✳ dictionary
- ✳ thesaurus
- ✳ encyclopedia
- ✳ calculator
- ✳ atlas

- ✳ image search
- ✳ translator
- ✳ metric converter
- ✳ temperature converter
- ✳ currency converter

All of these sources can be accessed with computers online or in more traditional paper and book form. The specific tools used for each story will depend on the story's content. A teacher should be prepared to be flexible when it comes to sources.

Stories can be read in any order.

Questions and Writing Practice

Standardized-test questions written in multiple-choice and true/false formats are included in varying directed research source sections. In addition, students are asked for short-answer and complete-sentence responses in many selections. Questions require a student to do the following:

✳ focus on and synthesize what he or she just researched

✳ apply his or her knowledge to questions in standardized test format.

A writing sample is asked for at the end of each story unit. The writing sample is expected to be about one paragraph in length, but it can vary depending on student ability. Many of the writing samples require that a student put together all the information that he or she has gathered and develop some type of conclusion or opinion. Often, the student is asked to use correct or incorrect facts from the story to support his or her conclusion. In other cases, the student may be asked to make up a short, fictional story or describe something from his or her own experience.

This type of writing exercise provides an opportunity for students to do the following:

✳ critically think about what they read

✳ form an opinion using information they have inferred or determined to be true or false

✳ combine logical reasoning and well-reasoned responses with writing mechanics.

Vocabulary

One vocabulary word is highlighted in each story and then used several times. Using a dictionary or thesaurus to do further research on the word is always required. The research may focus on definition, synonyms, antonyms, or usage. In addition, students are instructed to use the word (when appropriate) in their writing sample.

Highlighted vocabulary words are listed below. They are presented in the order in which they appear in the book.

1. atypical	**10.** fluctuate	**19.** unfathomable
2. benefit	**11.** fabrication	**20.** stellar
3. archaeology	**12.** frigid	**21.** remote
4. vast	**13.** iota	**22.** rash
5. vile	**14.** resume	**23.** aromatic
6. plummet	**15.** endemic	**24.** vendor
7. entranced	**16.** hardy	**25.** tenacious
8. stamina	**17.** verbose	
9. irk	**18.** pacific	

Each school has its own computer/internet acceptable-use policy. A teacher must make sure to have signed copies and permission slips from each student, or whatever their district requires. The following text may be reviewed with or handed out to the class.

Internet Safety

A hammer and a saw are valuable tools. Hammers and saws help make it possible to build houses, schools, and skateboard parks. What if we don't use these tools correctly?

If a hammer and a saw are not used correctly, we or others could get hurt. We think before using these tools. We decide when and how it is safe. For example, we do not use a hammer on a glass table. We do not try to saw a rope that is holding us up. We make sure that no one close to us can get hurt.

The internet is a valuable tool. Just like a hammer and a saw, the internet must be used correctly. You must think critically when you are using the internet. Before you click on a link, you must think: Is it safe or not safe? Before you write or post something, you must think: Will this information harm me or others in years to come?

There are many safety rules while using the internet. Each school has its own policy, too. You must always follow your school's policies as well as these top six safety rules:

1. **Ask questions!**

   Be near an adult so that you can ask questions and report anything suspicious.

2. **Keep private information to yourself!**

   Do not share your name, address, phone number, age, or school, and do not send a picture to anyone online.

   Keep other people's information private, too. This includes information about your friends and parents' workplaces, credit card numbers, addresses, or emails.

   Keep your passwords private. Combine uppercase, lowercase, and numbers when you make a password.

3. **Don't be tempted!**

   Do not enter contests, clubs, or chat rooms without adult permission.

4. **Do not keep secrets!**

   If someone asks to meet you somewhere, to talk on the phone, or for your picture, tell an adult immediately.

6. **Follow the laws!**

   Never send mail that could hurt someone or make them feel threatened now or in the future. What you post may stay on the World Wide Web for years! Never copy commercial files without permission. Never use other people's passwords.

Research Notes for Students

There will be one or two ways you can search for facts. Use the icons below to guide you to the right sources. You may use online sources or books, charts, and other reference materials.

Note: Sometimes the first site you go to may not give you the exact information you need. When this happens, try another site or a different reference book. When you do find a site that is especially helpful or easy to use, you may want to bookmark it or remember its address. That way you can quickly find it when you need it.

Search Engine and/or Encyclopedia

To find factual information on the internet about any topic, you can use an online encyclopedia. Type in "encyclopedia" and click on the encyclopedia of your choice. Another way to find this information would be to simply use a program called a search engine. These programs use key words to search the Web. *Google*, *Yahoo!*, and *Bing* are examples of search engines. Just go to one of these sites and type **key words** into a search box. For example, type in "13th US president" to find out who was the 13th president of the United States.

Dictionary

Use an online dictionary to find the definitions of words. Type "dictionary [word to be defined]" or "[word to be defined] definition" into a search engine.

Thesaurus

A thesaurus is used to find synonyms (same meanings) and antonyms (opposite meanings). Type in "[word] synonyms" or "[word] antonyms" or "thesaurus [word]."

Calculator

Use an online calculator for solving addition, subtraction, and other math problems. Type in the problem (for example, "1 + 6") or the word "calculator." There will be many sites with calculators. Find the one you like the best. An example of an appropriate site would be *http://calculator-1.com/*.

Atlas 	An atlas is a collection of maps. Go to a search engine and type in "atlas [name of place]" or "[name of place] map."
Image Search 	To find a picture of just about any person or thing, go to a search engine and type in the name of the person or thing and then the word "images." You will usually have several different images to look at and compare. (**Teacher Note:** Make sure settings are preset to filter out inappropriate images.)
Translator 	Type the word "translate" into a search engine box. Then choose the translation site you are most comfortable with.
Metric Converter 	Go to a search engine and type in "metric converter." Click on what you are converting from and to what. Plug in the numbers. An example site would be *http://www.worldwidemetric.com/measurements.html*.
Temperature Converter 	Go to a search engine and type in "temperature converter." Click on what you are converting from and to what. Plug in the numbers. An example site would be *http://www.onlineconversion.com/temperature.htm*.
Currency Converter 	Go to a search engine and type in "currency converter." Click on what you are converting from and to what. Plug in the numbers. An example site would be *http://www.xe.com/*.

Common Core State Standards

Each activity in 21st Century Fact Finds: Using Online Research Tools to Reinforce Common Core Skills meets one or more of the following Common Core State Standards. (© Copyright 2010. National Governors Association Center for Best Practices and Council of Chief State School Officers. All rights reserved.) For more information about the Common Core State Standards, go to *http://www.corestandards.org/*.

Informational Text Standards
Key Ideas and Details
Standard 1: RI.6.1. Cite textual evidence to support analysis of what the text says explicitly as well as inferences drawn from the text. **Standard 2:** RI.6.2. Determine a central idea of a text and how it is conveyed through particular details; provide a summary of the text distinct from personal opinions and judgments.
Craft and Structure
Standard 4: RI.6.4. Determine the meaning of words and phrases as they are used in a text, including figurative, connotative, and technical meanings.
Integration of Knowledge and Ideas
Standard 7: RI.6.7. Integrate information presented in different media or formats (e.g., visually, quantitatively) as well as words to develop a coherent understanding of a topic or issue. **Standard 8:** RI.6.8. Trace and evaluate the argument and specific claims in a text, distinguishing claims that are supported by reasons and evidence from claims that are not.
Range of Reading and Level of Text Complexity
Standard 10: RI.6.10. By the end of the year, read and comprehend literary nonfiction in the grades 6–8 text complexity band proficiently, with scaffolding as needed at the high end of the range.

Writing Standards
Text Types and Purposes
Standard 1: W.6.1. Write arguments to support claims with clear reasons and relevant evidence. • W.6.1a. Introduce claim(s) and organize the reasons and evidence clearly. • W.6.1b. Support claim(s) with clear reasons and relevant evidence, using credible sources and demonstrating an understanding of the topic or text. • W.6.1c. Use words, phrases, and clauses to clarify the relationships among claim(s) and reasons. • W.6.1e. Provide a concluding statement or section that follows from the arguments presented. **Standard 2:** W.6.2. Write informative/explanatory texts to examine a topic and convey ideas, concepts, and information through the selection, organization, and analysis of relevant content. **Standard 3:** W.6.3. Write narratives to develop real or imagined experiences or events using effective technique, relevant descriptive details, and well-structured event sequences.

Writing Standards *(cont.)*
Productions and Distribution of Writing
Standard 4: W.6.4. Produce clear and coherent writing in which the development, organization, and style are appropriate to task, purpose, and audience.
Research to Build and Present Knowledge
Standard 8: W.6.8. Gather relevant information from multiple print and digital sources; access the credibility of each source; and quote or paraphrase the data and conclusions of others while avoiding plagiarism and providing basic bibliographic information for sources. **Standard 9:** W.6.9. Draw evidence from literary or informational texts to support analysis, reflection, and research.

Language Standards
Conventions of Standard English
Standard 1: L.6.1. Demonstrate command of the conventions of standard English grammar and usage when writing or speaking. **Standard 2:** L.6.2. Demonstrate command of the conventions of standard English capitalization, punctuation, and spelling when writing. **Standard 4:** L.6.4. Determine or clarify the meaning of unknown and multiple-meaning words and phrases based on grade 6 reading and content, choosing flexibly from a range of strategies. • L.6.4a. Use context (e.g., the overall meaning of a sentence or paragraph; a word's position of function in a sentence) as a clue to the meaning of a word or phrase. • L.6.4b. Use common, grade-appropriate Greek or Latin affixes and roots as clues to the meaning of a word (e.g., audience, auditory, audible.) • L.6.4c. Consult reference materials (e.g., dictionaries, glossaries, thesauruses), both print and digital, to find the pronunciation of a word or determine or clarify its precise meaning or its part of speech. • L.6.4d. Verify the preliminary determination of the meaning of a word or phrase (e.g., by checking the inferred meaning in context or in a dictionary). **Standard 6:** L.6.6. Acquire and use accurately grade-appropriate general academic and domain-specific words and phrases; gather vocabulary knowledge when considering a word or phrase important to comprehension or expression.

"I know a place where the floors squeak," Justin said. "I know another place where the stairs aren't even."

Lucy said, "So what? There are lots of old dwellings and houses that have squeaky floors and uneven stairs. Dry boards naturally creak under pressure, and the boards in old staircases often warp with age."

"The floors were built to squeak," Justin said, "and the stairs are made of stone. The stairs were purposefully built with uneven steps."

Lucy thought for a moment, and then she asked, "What kind of dwellings were these? Are squeaky floors and uneven stairs typical or **atypical** features?"

Grinning, Justin said, "Those are excellent questions! The dwellings are castles, and the squeaky floors and uneven steps were typical features. They were not atypical at all." Justin went on to explain, "Castles in Japan were carefully built and designed so that some floors—typically the hallways—squeaked when walked upon. Actually, the sound is more like a chirp, and it's made by the flooring nails rubbing against some type of clamp. If an intruder tried to sneak in, the guards were alerted by the chirps. These floors are commonly known as nightingale floors."

"I didn't know there were castles in Japan," Lucy said.

"Japan has lots of castles," Justin said. "Castles are fortresses, and there are many styles. Perhaps the most famous example of one with a nightingale floor is Nijo Castle in Kyoto."

Justin continued, "A nightingale floor would be an atypical feature in a Medieval European stone castle, but the uneven stone steps are typical. The uneven steps were for defense, too. Stairwells were very dim, very narrow, and curved in a clockwise direction. That meant intruders typically had their sword hands against the interior curve of the wall because they were right-handed. This made it difficult for them to swing their swords, while the defenders coming down had more room."

"But what good were the uneven steps?" asked Lucy.

"That just added to the defender's advantage," Justin replied. "People who went up and down the steps all the time would know where every uneven step was. Intruders who weren't familiar with the steps could easily trip. Blarney Castle in Blarney has a stairwell which is a great example of this type of planned defense."

"Have you actually seen these features, or are you just making it all up?" asked Lucy.

"Oh, they're real, all right," Justin assured her. "In fact, I'm leaving tomorrow for the capital of Japan. I'll visit Nijo Castle in that city, and then I'll fly to the capital of Ireland where Blarney Castle is located. I'll bring you back photographs."

"I don't think that's possible," Lucy said.

What isn't possible? It is time to check facts.

Thesaurus

1. Name two synonyms for *atypical*. _____ _____

2. Now name two antonyms. _____ _____

3. Explain what removing the prefix *a* does to the word *atypical*.

_____

_____

Image Search

Key Words: (🔍 *Nijo Castle*)　(🔍 *Blarney Castle*)　(🔍 *Nightingale floor*)

1. Which of these castles appears to be constructed mostly of stone?

_____

_____

2. Which castle appears to be taller? _____

3. Do you think you could make a nightingale floor with stones? Explain.

_____

_____

(**Bonus:** If you go to *http://en.wikipedia.org/wiki/Nightingale_floor* you can see a picture of the underside of a nightingale floor and listen to someone walking on one.)

Search Engine/Encyclopedia

1. What is the capital of Japan? _____

2. What is the capital of Ireland? _____

3. What mistake did Justin make? (Hint: castle location) _____

_____

In Your Own Words

Think about where you live. If you could have a nightingale floor or a stairwell like in Blarney Castle, which one would you install? On a separate piece of paper, describe the features of your choice. Tell why you chose it, where you would put it, and why.

"I have found Tycho Brahe's lab notes," Professor Con said. "If you give me more money for research, I am sure that I can turn copper into gold. Your investment will **benefit** us both."

"Who is Tycho Brahe?" asked Susannah's father.

"Tycho Brahe was an astronomer and an alchemist. He was born in 1546 and died in 1601. He was from Denmark. He had an observatory and lab in Denmark's capital. That's where he made observations about the planets and tried to turn copper into gold," Professor Con answered.

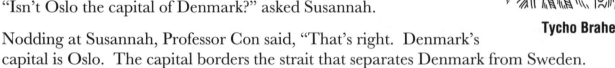

Tycho Brahe

"Isn't Oslo the capital of Denmark?" asked Susannah.

Nodding at Susannah, Professor Con said, "That's right. Denmark's capital is Oslo. The capital borders the strait that separates Denmark from Sweden.

"It was the King of Denmark himself who provided Brahe's research funds. You see, Brahe lost his nose in a duel so he had to wear a replacement one. He had a replacement made of copper, but there was a problem with it. Copper melts at 1,083° Celsius, and so when Brahe would stand in direct sun too long or stand close to a hot fire, his nose would begin to melt! Brahe wanted a gold nose because a gold nose wouldn't melt. The problem was the expense. It cost too much to make a nose out of gold. That's when Brahe began to work on turning copper into gold. The king funded Brahe's work because if Brahe could find a way to turn copper into gold, then it would benefit the king. He could become rich."

"Is changing copper into gold really a possibility," asked Susannah's father. "If Brahe couldn't do it, what makes you think you can?"

"I can," Professor Con said with confidence. "Brahe left a chemical formula and instructions. The problem was that he didn't have the lab equipment that we have today." Holding out a piece of old, yellowed paper Professor Con said, "Take a look."

Both Susannah and her father leaned over the page the professor was showing them and read, "1 Cu + 4 Ir + 6 H (melted) = Go."

Professor Con explained, "Every element has a symbol. 'Cu' is the symbol for copper, 'Ir' is the symbol for iron, 'H' is the symbol for hydrogen, and 'Go' is the symbol for gold. Hydrogen is a gas, and Brahe didn't have the equipment to melt it. That's because hydrogen's melting point is -259° Celsius."

Susannah's father said slowly, "Being able to turn copper into gold would be to my benefit, but I'm having a hard time believing any of this. Your tale of a nose cut off in a duel and replaced with a copper one is pretty far-fetched."

Susannah said, "Dad, that part is believable, but trust me, you will not benefit if you invest in Professor Con's research. He doesn't know what he is talking about."

What does Susannah know that her father doesn't? It is time to check facts.

Dictionary

1. If something benefits you, it _____.

2. Why might a school hold a benefit spaghetti dinner? _____

_____

Atlas

Find a map of Denmark. Write **True** or **False**. If your answer is **False**, cross out the incorrect word(s) and write the correct word(s) on the line.

_____ 1. Denmark's capital is Oslo. _____

_____ 2. The capital borders the strait that separates Denmark and Sweden.

_____

Image Search

Key Words: (🔍 *Tycho Brache nose*)

Can you tell if Brache found a replacement for his nose?   **Yes**   **No**

Temperature Converter

Find the melting points of copper and hydrogen in degrees Fahrenheit. Then tell how these temperatures compare to the temperature on a hot day.

		Celsius	Fahrenheit	How compares?
1.	Copper	1,083°		
2.	Hydrogen	−259°		

Search Engine/Encyclopedia

Look up the chemical symbols for the following:

1. Copper _____   3. Hydrogen _____

2. Iron _____   4. Gold _____

In Your Own Words

On a separate piece of paper, write one or two paragraphs in which you explain why someone should or should not invest in Professor Con's research. When you write, try to use the word *benefit* at least one time.

Christopher's uncle picked Christopher up from school. Christopher's uncle was very excited. "Look," he cried, "I just received this in the mail. It says that I've won a free trip to Jordan and a tour of Petra. All I have to do is put 500 dollars down to reserve my spot, but I'll be reimbursed when the trip is over. I hope you don't mind going with me to the address on the envelope so I can pay my money and reserve my spot."

As Christopher's uncle drove, he said, "Ever since I was a young child, I've always been interested in **archaeology**. Ancient ruins fascinate me, and Petra has fabulous ruins. Did you know that Petra was a lost city that wasn't discovered until 1812?"

"How can a city get lost?" asked Christopher.

"Oh, it was abandoned about 2,000 years ago, but in the 6th century BCE, it was the capital of the Nabataea kingdom and the center of the caravan trade," answered Christopher's uncle. "It's like a fortress, because its buildings are cut out of rock."

"That still doesn't explain how a city could get lost," Christopher said.

"Archaeologists believe that part of the reason it was abandoned is that there was a huge earthquake that crippled their water supply. Then people forgot about it because it wasn't easily seen," Christopher's uncle explained. "You see, the city is located on the edges of the Wadi Araba desert. It is 50 miles south of the Dead Sea. The only way you can enter is through a long, narrow crevice. The crevice is only about five meters wide, and on both sides, there are towering sandstone walls hundreds of feet high."

"Sounds like the trip of a lifetime," Christopher said, as he and his uncle located the office that matched the address on the envelope.

Inside the office, there was a woman working. When Christopher's uncle showed her his letter, she said, "You can sign this paper and pay me now. Don't worry. You will get your money back. You will be reimbursed as soon as we land in Amman. Amman is the capital of Jordon, and that is where our hotel is located. The archaeologist who will be guiding us through Petra will meet us there."

"What does this say?" asked Christopher's uncle as he looked at the paper.

"Oh," said the woman laughing. "It is written in Arabic. Here, I'll read it and translate it into English as I go." She put her finger under the first word on the top left of the page. As she ran her finger across the page to the right, she said, "This payment of 500 dollars reserves my spot. I will be reimbursed at the end of the trip. I will not write graffiti on or otherwise harm this archaeological wonder."

"Sounds good to me," Christopher's uncle said as he picked up a pen.

"Wait," Christopher said suddenly. "You can't trust what's on the paper."

Christopher's uncle said, "Do you know how to read Arabic?"

"No," said Christopher, "but I'm not sure everyone is being honest here. I wouldn't give 500 dollars or even 500 dinars to this person."

What does Christopher know that is uncle doesn't? It is time to check facts.

Dictionary

1. What is archaeology the study of? _____

2. An archaeologist would most likely be interested in

   Ⓐ narrow crevices   Ⓒ ancient cities

   Ⓑ being reimbursed   Ⓓ recent earthquakes

Image Search

Key Words: 🔍 *Petra Jordan*   🔍 *Petra Jordan entrance*

Write down a few adjectives or words to describe Petra's. . .

   1. buildings: _____

   2. entrance: _____

Atlas

   1. Is Petra south of the Dead Sea? _____

   2. Is Amman the capital of Jordan? _____

Search Engine/Encyclopedia

Key Words: 🔍 *in what direction is Arabic read?*

Circle the direction in which Arabic is read.

    left to right   or   **right to left**

Currency Converter

What is 500 Jordanian dinars (JOD) worth in U.S. dollars? _____

In Your Own Words

On a separate piece of paper, write a paragraph in which you explain why Christopher doesn't think the woman is being honest. Include some reasons why Christopher's uncle might not have been suspicious.

"Our guest speaker Dr. Vasto will arrive shortly," Ms. Ming said to the class. "Dr. Vasto is from Argentina, and he is going to tell us about an animal that is native to a particular region of his country. In the few minutes before he arrives, I'd like to know what you students know about Argentina."

"Argentina is in South America," Jamie said. "It's not the largest country in the world, but it's the largest country in South America. It's the largest Spanish-speaking country in the world, too."

"Its capital is Buenos Aires. It is bordered by the Pacific Ocean to the south and east. Its country neighbors are Chile, Bolivia, Paraguay, and Uruguay," Amy said.

Before anyone could say anything more, Dr. Vasto arrived. "*Estoy muy contento de estar aquí hoy*," Dr. Vasto said. "I'm going to tell you about a very unique and special amphibian. This amphibian lives in the Pampas region. The Pampas region is a **vast** area made up of flat, fertile grasslands. These vast plains are located in central and eastern Argentina."

Dr. Vasto continued, "This amphibian weighs 27 to 64 kilograms. It has a body length of 100 to 120 centimeters. Its tail measures 70 to 90 centimeters. That's a long tail, but this amphibian uses it in a unique way. It uses it like a bicycle kickstand to balance on two legs! It uses its long, tubular snout in a unique way, too. It uses it as a snorkel as it swims."

"What in the world could he be talking about?" whispered Jamie to Amy.

"I'm talking about an animal that doesn't have any teeth," Dr. Vasto said with a smile. "It has a tongue that looks like a strand of spaghetti. It's about 60 centimeters long. The tongue has tiny, backward-pointing spines that are covered in sticky saliva. It eats a vast number of ants and termites every day. It eats up to 30,000!"

"Could it be a giant anteater?" asked Amy in a puzzled voice.

"Yes!" Dr. Vasto said. "It is the *oso hormiguero*. When this animal feeds, it may dart its tongue into an ant mound 150 times per minute! Then, after a minute, it moves onto another ant mound. This way, despite the vast number of ants it eats, it never wipes out the population."

After Dr. Vasto left, Jamie asked, "Why didn't Dr. Vasto use inches and pounds?"

"Argentina uses the metric system," Ms. Ming answered. "Most countries do."

Amy said, "That explains the centimeters and kilograms, but there's another word Dr. Vasto used that I'm not sure is correct."

Ms. Ming started to laugh. Then she said, "So our guest said something that was incorrect, but so did Amy and Jamie."

What was said that was incorrect? It is time to check facts.

Thesaurus

1. What are three synonyms for *vast*?

   _____ _____ _____

2. Name one thing you would describe as vast. _____

Atlas

Check what was said about Argentina. Write **True** or **False**. If your answer is **False**, cross out the incorrect word(s) and write the correct word(s) on the line.

_____ 1. Argentina's capital is Buenos Aires. _____

_____ 2. Argentina is the largest country in South America. _____

_____ 3. It is bordered by the Pacific Ocean. _____

Translator *(from Spanish to English)*

1. *Estoy muy contento de estar aquí hoy.* _____

2. *oso hormiguero* _____

3. Did Dr. Vasto mean to say *anfibio* or *mamífero*? _____

Metric Converter

What are the anteater's measurements in standard units?

1. Length: 100 to 120 centimeters =   _____ to _____ _____

2. Tail: 70 to 90 centimeters =   _____ to _____ _____

3. Tongue: 60 centimeters =   _____ _____

Image Search

Key Words: 🔍 *giant anteater tongue*

Describe the anteater's tongue. _____

In Your Own Words

Imagine you are visiting a school in Argentina and speaking about an animal from your country. On a separate piece of paper, write one paragraph in which you describe the animal. Think about what it looks like, where it lives, what it eats, and its behavior.

Inspector Crane looked carefully around the scene of the crime. Millions of dollars' worth of diamonds had been stolen from the bank's vault. The bank was located in Albany, New York. There had been a rash of similar thefts in other banks, and Inspector Crane believed that the same mastermind was behind all of the robberies. "It's Vinnie Vile," Inspector Crane said.

"Two questions," Police Officer Grackle said. "First, does the name fit? Second, if this looks like one of Vile's jobs, why hasn't he been arrested yet?"

Inspector Crane said, "Vinnie Vile is indeed **vile**, so yes, the name fits. Vile's behavior is nasty and criminal, but that doesn't mean he isn't smart. Vile hasn't been caught yet because he always has the perfect alibi. He has always been able to prove he was elsewhere during the time of the crime."

Police Officer Grackle said, "The security tapes show that the theft occurred between 2:00 and 3:00 P.M. Sunday afternoon. So let's go see what Vile was doing then."

"I was talking on my phone to my friend in Wellington, New Zealand," Vinnie Vile said to Inspector Crane and Police Officer Grackle when they questioned him. "My friend is an ornithologist whose main interest of study is the kiwi."

"You were talking to someone about a bird?" asked Police Officer Grackle in disbelief.

"That's right," Vinnie Vile said. "I was talking on a landline phone in this house. Check the records." Smugly grinning, Vile continued, "The kiwi is an amazing bird. It's flightless, and it's found only in New Zealand. It's got a really long beak, and it's the only bird with nostrils at the end of its beak. This means that it can locate worms and other insects underground without even seeing or feeling them. It just sticks its nose into the ground and smells them! The kiwi is also famous for its eggs. The kiwi is only about the size of a chicken, but its eggs are almost as big as an emu's eggs! A kiwi's eggs are one of the largest in proportion to body of any bird in the world. Just one egg may weigh 20 percent of the mother's weight! Call my friend in New Zealand. He'll tell you what we were talking about on Sunday between 2:00 and 3:00 P.M."

Inspector Crane called New Zealand. Vinnie Vile's friend said, "Yes, I am an ornithologist. I study birds, and my specialty is the kiwi. Did you know that the kiwi's body temperature is 38 degrees Celsius, which is more like a mammal than a bird."

"Enough bird facts," Inspector Crane cut in. "What time were you talking to Vinnie Vile?"

"Between 2:00 and 3:00 P.M. on Sunday," was the quick reply. "I remember exactly because two other ornithologists were here. Both of them will tell you they were here on Sunday afternoon and heard me converse with Vinnie."

Police Officer Grackle was listening in. He said, "I don't need to hear anything more. I've got enough information to discredit Vinnie Vile's alibi!"

What did Police Officer Grackle hear that makes him so sure? It is time to check facts.

Thesaurus

1. What is not a synonym for *vile*?

Ⓐ disgusting   Ⓑ evil   Ⓒ kind   Ⓓ revolting

2. What is one food or dish you consider to be vile? _____

Image Search

Key Words: 🔍 *kiwi bird*

Draw the outline of a kiwi's head and beak.

Temperature Converter

Is 38 degrees Celsius close to the average human temperature (98.6°F)?   **Yes**   **No**

Calculator

1. If a kiwi's egg weighs 20% of its body weight, how much would the egg weigh if the bird weighs 10 pounds?

Ⓐ 1 pound   Ⓑ 2 pounds   Ⓒ 5 pounds   Ⓓ 20 pounds

2. If a person could lay an egg that was 20% of his or her body weight, how big would the egg be if the person weighed 105 pounds?

Ⓐ 10.5 pounds   Ⓑ 15 pounds   Ⓒ 21 pounds   Ⓓ 25 pounds

Search Engine/Encyclopedia

1. What is the current time and date in Wellington, New Zealand? _____

_____

2. What is the current time and date in Albany, New York? _____

_____

In Your Own Words

Do you think Police Officer Grackle can discredit Vinny Vile's alibi? On a separate piece of paper, write a paragraph in which you explain why or why not. Then, give some reasons why at first one might think Vinnie's friend was completely honest.

Falling Faster than Sound

"On October 14, 2012, a man was able to **plummet** faster than the speed of sound," Michele said.

"I don't think that's possible," responded Dallas.

"Oh, it had already been done," Michele said. "On August 16, 1960, Joseph Kittinger rode in a balloon-propelled open gondola to an altitude of 102,800 feet. That's 19.5 miles above the Earth. That was so high that if Kittinger didn't wear a special suit, the liquid in his body would have turned to gas! As it was, there was a malfunction in the right glove of the suit, so Kittinger's hand swelled up to twice its size! Kittinger jumped out and plummeted for four minutes and 36 seconds. He reached a speed of 614 miles per hour. It wasn't until he was at 18,000 feet that he opened his parachute."

Dallas shook his head in disbelief. He said, "I just can't believe it."

Michele said, "It's true, and a man named Felix Baumgartner went even faster in 2012! Baumgartner jumped from a fiberglass sphere once it rose to over 120,000 feet above the Earth's surface. He plummeted for four minutes and 19 seconds, which was just 17 seconds less than Kittinger's record. However, Baumgartner reached a top speed of over 843 miles per hour! That beat Kittinger's record by a lot."

Michele continued, "Baumgartner's suit was much more advanced than Kittinger's. It was a pressure suit that had been designed by space-suit specialists. It was much more maneuverable than Kittinger's suit."

Dallas was silent for a moment. Then he said, "I'm still not sure I believe you. Felix Baumgartner is a famous BASE jumper. I've never heard of him doing high-altitude jumps."

"What's a BASE jumper?" asked Michele.

"BASE jumping is a sport in which you jump from fixed objects. BASE is an acronym. It stands for the four categories of fixed objects from which one can jump. The B stands for buildings. The A stands for antennas. The S stands for spans, like bridges, and the E stands for earth, like cliffs. Baumgartner holds world titles for his BASE jumping. He has jumped 1,669 feet down from the Taipei 101 Tower in Taipei, Taiwan. He jumped 1,125 feet from the Millau Bridge in France. He even holds the world record for the lowest BASE jump. He set that record when he jumped 95 feet from a statue in Rio de Janeiro, Brazil."

"No one could jump from 95 feet and have time to deploy a parachute and survive," Michele said. "What I said is possible, but what you said is impossible."

What is possible and what is impossible? It is time to check facts.

Dictionary

1. What is the meaning of *plummet*? _____

2. In one or two sentences describe a time when you plummeted or felt like you were plummeting to the ground. Were you on a bike or roller skates, did you trip, or something else?

   _____

   _____

Calculator

1. Since 5,280 feet = 1 mile, how many miles above Earth is 102,800 feet?

   _____

2. How much faster did Baumgartner go than Kittinger? _____ mph

Image Search

Key Words: 🔍 *Joseph Kittingner jump*   🔍 *Felix Baumgartner jump*

Which man's suit looks easier to move in? Explain. _____

_____

Search Engine/ Encyclopedia

Key Words: 🔍 *speed of sound*

1. The speed of sound is about _____ miles per hour.

2. Did Kittinger plummet faster than the speed of sound?   **Yes**   **No**

3. Has Baumgartner BASE jumped from the following places? _____

   a. Taipei Tower, Taiwan   **Yes**   **No**

   b. Millau Bridge, France   **Yes**   **No**

   c. Christos Statue, Rio de Janeiro, Brazil   **Yes**   **No**

In Your Own Words

What do you think Kittinger and Baumgartner thought and felt right before jumping and during their fall? Imagine you are one of them. On a separate piece of paper, write a paragraph in which you describe all of your inner thoughts during a jump.

"I just received this invitation to an art auction," Claire's elderly neighbor Mrs. Marseille said. "Look at the painting on the back of the invitation. That is the one I want to buy. I've always wanted to purchase an old French masterpiece, and I was **entranced** by this one the minute I saw it. In the paragraph underneath the picture of the painting, it says it was painted in 1422 by a man who lived in Paris. His studio was at the edge of the city, right where the Seine River meets the Mediterranean Sea. Can you imagine owning something so old and charming?"

Claire looked at the picture Mrs. Marseille was interested in. It was of a barefoot woman dressed as a 15th century French peasant. A white scarf covered her head, and she wore an apron over her long skirt. The woman was sitting on the ground with her wares spread around her. She had a basket of potatoes to her left, corn to her right, and bunches of bright-yellow sunflowers spread out in front of her. The

colors and lines of the painting were charming, and Claire could see why the pastoral scene had entranced her elderly neighbor.

"Claire," Mrs. Marseille said, "as long as you are holding the invitation, you can help me. Tell me what number to call to reserve my place at the auction."

Claire said, "There's lots of phone numbers here. How do I know which one you are supposed to call?"

"Why, the one following the letters 'RSVP' of course," Mrs. Marseille said. "The letters 'RSVP' come from the French *répondre, s'il vous plaît*. Whenever those letters are at the end of an invitation, it is proper etiquette to reply and inform the host if one can accept the invitation. It's more than being polite. It also helps the host plan for the event because he or she will know how many people to expect."

Mrs. Marseille continued, "Really, *chérie*, you should learn to speak French. I have always been entranced by French art and culture, and that is why I studied French in school. Is there any French phrase you would like to learn right now?"

Claire looked once more at the invitation, and then she said, "I think you should teach me how to say, "No, thank you."

"*Mais pourquoi?*" demanded Mrs. Marseille.

"Because," Claire said, "As entrancing as this painting may be, it could not have been painted in 1422. And as for the artist, I don't know if his studio was actually in Paris or not, but one certainly can't use what is written on this invitation to locate it."

Why is Claire so sure Mrs. Marseille should not buy the painting? It is time to check facts.

Thesaurus

1. Write two synonyms for *entranced*. _____ _____

2. Write two antonyms for *entranced*. _____ _____

3. What might entrance a kitten? _____

_____

Atlas

Write **True** or **False** for each of these statements from the story. If your answer is **False**, cross out the incorrect word(s) and write the correct word(s) on the line.

_____ **1.** Paris is in France. _____

_____ **2.** The Seine runs into the Mediterranean Sea. _____

Translator *(from French to English)*

1. *répondre, s'il vous plaît* _____

2. *chérie* _____

3. *Mais pourquoi?* _____

4. How would you write the sentence, "No, thank you," in French?

_____

Search Engine/Encyclopedia

1. What years are in the 15th century? _____

2. Where did corn originate? _____

3. Where did potatoes originate? _____

4. Where did sunflowers originate? _____

In Your Own Words

On a separate piece of paper, draft a paragraph that will serve as Mrs. Marseille's RSVP. (You choose if she accepts or declines.) In your paragraph, discuss the artist's studio. Explain, too, why the painting could not have been painted in France in 1422. (Hint: When did Europeans first sail to the Americas?)

The Highest Mountain

Laura said, "I am going to climb the highest mountain in the world."

Darren's jaw dropped in surprise. He said, "Wow! That will be some feat. Are you sure you have enough stamina to make it up the mountain?"

"Of course I have enough **stamina**," laughed Laura. "My dad is going to drive a rental car up to the trailhead, and then we will hike the six miles up the summit. We don't have to worry about getting lost because there are iron poles marking the path every 152 meters, but we do have to bring lots of water and sunscreen because there are no amenities along the trail."

Shaking his head, Darren said, "Of course there are no amenities on the top of the highest mountain. The trail is snowy, icy, and extremely hazardous. The top third of it is in the death zone. That's where the air is so thin that there is not enough oxygen to survive. Most climbers breathe bottled oxygen, but still, they have to be in great physical condition to have enough stamina for the climb."

"We won't need bottled oxygen," laughed Laura, "and we don't have to worry about ice or snow, because we're going in the summer. We're expecting temperatures around 15 degrees Celsius, so we'll be fine."

"I'm not familiar with the Celsius scale," Darren said, "but I think your information is incorrect. On a good summit day, the temperature is -15° Fahrenheit. Note that that's on a good summit day! Other times, the temperature on the summit is a chilling -100° Fahrenheit!"

"No," Laura said, "I know my information is correct. In fact, we were told that the coldest it ever gets—and that's at night in the winter—is around -4° Celsius. That's not anywhere close to -100° Fahrenheit!"

Darren slowly shook his said and said, "I don't think you are going to be climbing the highest mountain. At 29,029 feet, Mount Everest is the highest mountain. Everest is part of the Andes mountain range, and it borders Nepal and Bhutan."

Laura said, "I'm not going to be climbing Everest! I'll be climbing Mauna Kea! My dad wants to visit all the observatories there. Mauna Kea is located on Hawaii's island of Oahu. When I stand on Mauna Kea's peak, I will be at 4,205 meters above sea level, and I will most definitely be on the top of the highest mountain in the world."

"That's not possible," Darren retorted. "29,029 feet is at least 10,000 feet higher than 4,205 meters. Mount Everest is the highest mountain in the world."

Who is right, Laura or Darren? It is time to check facts.

Thesaurus

1. Write down two synonyms for *stamina*. _____ _____

2. Explain how a mountain climber needs both mental and physical stamina.

   _____

   _____

Temperature Converter

1. Mount Everest summit:

Warmest	-15°F = °C
Coldest	-100°F = °C

2. Mauna Kea:

Warmest	15°C = °F
Coldest	-4°C = °F

Metric Converter

Show the peak heights above sea level in meters and feet for both mountains.

1. Mt. Everest: 29,029 feet = _____ meters

2. Mauna Kea (visible peak): _____ feet = 4,205 meters

Atlas

Write **True** or **False**. If your answer is **False**, cross out the incorrect word(s) and write the correct word(s) on the line.

_____ 1. Mount Everest is part of the Andes mountain range. _____

_____ 2. Mount Everest borders Nepal and Bhutan. _____

_____ 3. Mauna Kea is in Hawaii on the island of Oahu. _____

Image Search

Which mountain has observatories on its summit?

Mt. Everest   Mauna Kea

In Your Own Words

Which mountain do you think is the tallest in the world? On a separate piece of paper, state your opinion and then defend it. In your paragraph, tell where the mountain is located. Also, tell why others might disagree with you.

Grim, the Great White Shark

"You know what really **irks** me?" demanded Ellie. "I'm really irked by newspaper articles that aren't factual. There's nothing more irksome than reading something you know can't be true. Here, look at this article that was in today's newspaper." Chou carefully read the article that Ellie handed to him.

Great White Shark's Tropical Voyage

Grim is a 2.8-meter Great White shark that went on an epic tropical voyage. Grim's voyage started at Stewart Island, New Zealand. He then traveled to Fiji, Tonga, and Niue before heading home.

Scientists used a long pole to tag Grim with a $5,000 chip. The chip was drilled into Grim's first dorsal fin. The chip stores data on depth, temperature, and light levels. It provides accurate position data to 350 meters every time it breaks the surface. In just the first 11 days after Grim was tagged, he astounded scientists by traveling 1,200 kilometers.

How did Grim find his way home after his epic journey? Scientists are still learning how sharks migrate. Data from Grim's chip showed that he spent over half of his time swimming at the surface. Sharks have eyesight that is sensitive to dim light. Scientists think Grim may have used visual cues, such as the location of the sun or moon, to navigate. Alternatively, Grim may have used currents and Earth's magnetic field to orient himself.

"I think this article is fascinating," Chou told Ellie. "What parts bother you?"

"I told you," Ellie, said. "I'm irked by reporters that don't check their facts. I've heard of New Zealand and Fiji, but I've never heard of Tonga or Niue. I don't think those places exist. Second, I don't think it possible that a shark of that size could travel over 100 kilometers a day."

Chou replied, "I happen to know that nine-foot Great White sharks can easily travel 70 miles in a day. I also know that Tonga and Niue, like Fiji, are island nations in the South Pacific Ocean. Fiji is about 1,100 nautical miles northeast of New Zealand's North Island. Tonga is about 400 nautical miles southeast of Fiji. Niue is about 340 nautical miles east of Tonga. Unlike Fiji and Tonga, Niue is just one tiny island. It's about 100 square miles and has a population of about 1,300 people. Niue is self-governing, but it is associated with New Zealand. They lack full sovereignty so they are New Zealand citizens and use New Zealand dollars."

"Want to know what irks me now?" asked Ellie laughing. "What bothers me is my lack of knowledge. I don't know what nine feet is in meters. I don't know what 70 miles a day is in kilometers. I especially find it irksome that I don't know what a nautical mile is. Is a nautical mile the same as a mile? Until I know these things, I can't check your facts."

"I'll bet you 50 New Zealand dollars that my facts are correct," Chou said. "I'll bet you an additional 50 Fijian dollars that Grim is a real shark. I'll even bet you 50 Tongan pa'angas that the newspaper article is accurate, too."

Should Ellie take any of Chou's bets? It is time to check facts.

Dictionary

1. What is the meaning of *irk*? _____

2. Which of these sounds might be irksome when you are trying to sleep?

   Ⓐ a wind blowing   Ⓑ a rain falling   Ⓒ a horn honking

Metric Converter

Chou said a nine-foot shark could travel 70 miles a day. Could Grim?

1. Grim's length = 2.8 meters = _____ feet

2. Sharks can travel 70 miles per day, which equals _____ kilometers.

Atlas

Was Chou right when he said the following:

1. Fiji is northeast of New Zealand.   **Yes**   **No**

2. Tonga is southeast of Fiji.   **Yes**   **No**

3. Niue is east of Tonga.   **Yes**   **No**

Search Engine/Encyclopedia

Key Words: 🔍 *Grim Great White*   🔍 *nautical mile*

1. Is there a shark named Grim?   **Yes**   **No**

2. 1 nautical mile = _____ miles = _____ kilometers

Currency Converter *(convert to U.S. dollars)*

1. 500 New Zealand dollars (NZD) = _____ U.S. dollars (USD)

2. 500 Fijian dollars (FJD) = _____ U.S. dollars (USD)

3. 500 Tongan pa'angas (TOP) = _____ U.S. dollars (USD)

In Your Own Words

On a separate piece of paper, write a paragraph or two in which you contrast where you live to life on Niue. Think about Niue's size, location, and population. Describe some advantages and disadvantages to living in Niue. Would you like to live there?

Home to a Hospital and Blind Fish

"There is a place in Kentucky that was once home to a hospital and blind fish," Dana said.

"You mean it was a veterinary hospital?" asked Brian.

"No," Dana corrected Brian. "The hospital was for people. It was for TB patients. *TB* stands for *tuberculosis*."

"And why would a tuberculosis hospital be where there are blind fish?" asked Brian.

"Because," Dana replied, "the hospital was subterranean! It was built under the ground! The hospital was constructed far away from the air and light of the outside world. It was deep inside Mammoth Cave. Mammoth Cave is one of the world's largest cave systems. The cave is about 400 feet deep and has over 390 miles of passageways that have been explored and mapped. Some of the passages are really narrow, but the longest one extends all the way under Kentucky's neighboring state of Arkansas. There are also five levels of subterranean rooms, deep shafts, and underground rivers."

Dana continued, "And it's very dark in the cave. How dark? Put your hand in front of your face, and you can't see it. Eyes aren't necessary because there is no light to see anything anyways. The blind fish that live in the cave's waters are actually eyeless. They are a ghostly white, too, because over time they stopped developing unnecessary skin pigments as well as eye structures."

"That explains the blind fish," Brian said, "but it doesn't explain why the hospital was constructed there."

Dana answered, "The hospital was built inside the cave because of the cave's internal temperature. Outside, depending on the season, temperatures **fluctuate**. They can range from zero up to 90° Fahrenheit. Inside the cave however, the temperature barely fluctuates. It stays more or less at about 54° Fahrenheit. In the passageways close to the surface, it may fluctuate as much as 6 degrees up or down, but the hospital was built deep inside where temperatures were steady and didn't fluctuate.

"The hospital was built in the 1840s. At that time, people didn't know how to cure TB. They thought the constant, cool temperature and dry air of the cave would help them. Can you imagine being so ill and desperate to live that you would voluntarily descend for months into the dark depths of a cave? Of course, today we know that TB is a kind of skin cancer. People just needed to get away from the sun's light. Brian, I hope you protect yourself from too much sun. Do you wear long sleeves or use sun block?"

Brian said, "Dana, I don't think wearing long sleeves or using sun block will protect me from TB. Are you sure you have all your facts right? Do you have the correct location of your subterranean hospital?"

Home to a Hospital and Blind Fish *(cont.)*

Does Dana know what causes TB and where the hospital is located? It is time to check facts.

Dictionary

1. What is the meaning of *fluctuate*? _____

2. Which answer is an example of fluctuating?

Ⓐ No, I won't go.

Ⓑ Yes, I will go.

Ⓒ I will tell you tomorrow if I will go.

Ⓓ I'll go. Wait, no, I won't. Well, maybe."

Atlas

How many states does Kentucky border? Circle the correct answer.

4   5   6   7   8

Image Search

Key Words: 🔍 *eyeless fish*   🔍 *Mammoth Cave*

1. Do the eyeless fish have stripes?   **Yes   No**

2. Are they mostly light colored?   **Yes   No**

Temperature Converter

Mammoth Cave's temperature is about 54°F. That equals about . . .

Ⓐ 12°C   Ⓑ 14°C   Ⓒ 54°C   Ⓓ 129°C

Search Engine/Encyclopedia

Write **True** or **False**. If your answer is **False**, cross out the incorrect word(s) and write the correct word(s) on the line.

_____ **1.** Tuberculosis is a kind of skin cancer. _____

_____ **2.** Wearing long sleeves protects one from TB. _____

_____ **3.** Doctors use antibiotics to treat TB. _____

In Your Own Words

On a separate piece of paper, explain why Brian may have found it hard to believe that a hospital had been built in Mammoth Cave. Use your personal feelings, as well as some of the incorrect things Ellie said to support your answer.

"Look at what my mother received yesterday," Rosie said to Fabian as she handed him a letter. Its envelope had four stamps—two with pictures of Queen Elizabeth, one with a picture of Buckingham Palace, and one with a picture of Tower Bridge. The queen stamps were marked $9.14, and the others were marked $6.76 and $8.48." "That's a lot of postage," Fabian said.

"I added up the amount, and it comes to 32 dollars and 25 cents," Rosie said. "It cost so much because it was registered, insured, and came from England. My mom had to sign for it."

"Are you sure?" asked Fabian doubtfully as he read the letter.

10 Downing Street
London SW1A 2AA
United Kingdom
5-11-2012

Dear Elizabeth,

*I am sitting down on this day in May to inform you that I am your long-lost relative. This is not a **fabrication**. I would not fabricate such a tale, for I am a woman of honor. You see, I recently traced my ancestors back 200 years by looking through public records. I found out that my grandmother was your grandmother's older sister Rosalind. When your great-grandparents moved to the U.S., Rosalind was too sick to travel so they left her with your great-grandmother's sister. Your great-grandmother's sister wanted to raise Rosalind, so she wrote your great-grandparents and told them Rosalind had died. Then she took Rosalind and moved away deep into the English moorlands.*

I know this sounds like a wild tale, but it's the truth. I would love to visit you. Unfortunately, I was just recently run over by a lorry and so I can no longer walk up stairs. My flat building didn't have a lift, so I had to move into a more expensive building Wire money to the bank account listed on the back of this page, and I will buy my ticket and visit you.

Your long-lost relative,
Eliza Doolittle

"You know this letter is a complete and total fabrication," Fabian said as he finished reading it.

Rosie said, "My grandmother always said she had a sister who had died young."

"This letter didn't come from England," Fabian repeated.

Rosie said, "What makes you so sure it's fabricated? I did some checking, and the words in the letter make sense. In England, a lorry is a truck, a lift is an elevator, and certain parts of the countryside are referred to as moorlands!"

"Think about the stamps, the address, and the date," Fabian replied.

"I looked on a map," Rosie said, "and there is a 10 Downing Street, a Buckingham Palace, and a Tower Bridge that crosses the River Thames. As for the date, May is the 5th month everywhere in the world. Fabian, I'm sure this letter is authentic."

What does Fabian know that Rosie doesn't? It is time to check facts.

Dictionary

1. A fabrication is _____

2. When you fabricate something, you

   Ⓐ discover it.   Ⓑ remove it.   Ⓒ tear it up.   Ⓓ make it up.

Calculator

Use a calculator to add up the price of the stamps.

1. How much were the stamps? (2 x \$9.14) + 6.76 + 8.48 = \$ _____

2. Did Rosie have the correct postage amount?   **Yes   No**

Search Engine/Encyclopedia

1. Who lives at 10 Downing Street? _____

2. Who lives at Buckingham Palace? _____

3. How is the date written in Great Britain? Circle the correct choice.

   day-month-year   month-day-year

4. What river does the Tower Bridge cross? _____

Image Search

Key Words: 🔍 *British currency symbol*   🔍 *moorlands*

1. Find the currency of Great Britain.
   Draw its symbol in the box to the right.

2. Are moorlands heavily forested?   **Yes   No**

In Your Own Words

On a separate piece of paper, write a paragraph in which you explain why it is important to know how the date is written (dd-mm-yy or mm-dd-yy). In your paragraph, explain how your birthday and at least one other person's birthday would be written in the U.S. and Great Britain. Finally, tell if you think there should be one world system for writing dates.

Daniel and Rebecca wanted an adventure. They decided to spin a globe and move a finger in circles on the globe. When the globe stopped spinning, they would visit the place their finger was on. Using this method, they found their travel destination: Oymyakon.

Daniel and Rebecca could see from the globe that Oymyakon was located in Russia, but beyond that, they knew nothing about it. Deciding it would be wise to use a guide, they called a tour guide agency for the name of someone they might hire. They were given two phone numbers, and when they called the first one, a man named Mr. Zimin answered the phone.

"Yes, I know Oymyakon well," Mr. Zimin said. "Oymyakon is a small village above the Arctic Circle. It is directly north of Russia's capital, Moscow. Oymyakon is known for its cold and **frigid** temperatures. In fact, Oymyakon is the coldest permanently inhabited place on Earth. How frigid is it? Throw boiling water into the air, and it instantly freezes. The average winter temperature is -45 degrees Celsius. The lowest temperature ever recorded for any permanently inhabited location on Earth was measured here. What did the temperature measure on that record-breaking day? It measured a frigid -71.2 degrees Celsius!"

Mr. Zimin continued, "I speak Russian, so of course I can translate everything for you. I can also help you find lodging. It's such a small village that there aren't a lot of lodging options, and most likely you'll have to stay with a local family."

"But how can anyone survive in such a frigid environment?" asked Rebecca.

"People learn to adapt," Mr. Zimin explained. "People live in larch wood houses and burn coal and wood for heat. They breed reindeer, hunt, and ice-fish. People eat reindeer and horsemeat, and they wear fur to stay warm. Reindeer fur is particularly good at keeping you warm because the shaft of each hair is hollow, and the air in the shafts has an insulating effect."

"Do children there use cell phones and go to school the same as they do in warmer places?" asked Daniel.

"There's a single school, and it only closes when temperatures fall below -52 degrees Celsius. 2008 was the year that the school got an indoor toilet. Cell phones don't work in such frigid environments, and metal sticks to skin. Even ink in pens freezes solid!"

Daniel was silent for a minute, and then he asked, "If we hire you, can you find us reindeer clothes to wear?"

"Definitely," replied Mr. Zimin. "I'll even teach you how to say the word *reindeer* and *cold* in Russian. First, though, you need to send me some money."

Daniel said to Rebecca, "I think we should go ahead and hire Mr. Zimin.

"I disagree," Rebecca replied. "I'd rather call the second name on the list and see if that guide actually knows where Oymyakon is."

What does Rebecca know that Daniel doesn't? It is time to check facts.

Thesaurus

1. List two synonyms for *frigid*. _____   _____

2. Should a new student to your class be given a frigid welcome? Explain in one or two sentences. Use the word *frigid* at least once in your answer.

_____

_____

Atlas

1. Is Moscow the capital city of Russia?   **Yes**   **No**

2. Is Oymyakon directly north of Moscow?   **Yes**   **No**

3. Is Oymyakon above the Arctic Circle?   **Yes**   **No**

Temperature Converter

What are the temperatures in Oymyakon in Fahrenheit?

1. Average winter day: -45°C = _____ °F

2. School closes: -52°C = _____ °F

3. Record cold: -71.2°C = _____ °F

Translator (from English to Russian)

Find out how these words are pronounced in Russian. Do your best to write this pronunciation out.

1. reindeer: _____

2. cold: _____

Search Engine/Encyclopedia

1. Are reindeer hairs hollow?   **Yes**   **No**

2. Name one other animal with hollow hairs. _____

In Your Own Words

Image you are trying to get yourself hired as a guide for your area. What could you tell someone about where you live? On a separate piece of paper, describe some places of interest you could take them.

The Practical Ancient Wonder

"Do you believe in time travel?" Kelly's little sister Anna asked.

"Of course not," Kelly replied. "Whenever I read a story about time travel, I know that it hasn't an **iota** of truth in it."

"Not even the smallest, teensiest bit?" asked Anna.

"Since time travel is impossible, there can't be an iota of truth about it," Kelly said with great assurance.

"I thought you'd feel that way, and that's why I've brought back proof. Since none of the Seven Wonders of the Ancient World are standing today, I wanted to visit at least one. I chose the Great Lighthouse of Alexandria because it was the only wonder that had a practical purpose. The lighthouse was built on the island of Pharos in Alexandria, Egypt. It was built around 280 to 247 BC. It was the world's first lighthouse, and its purpose was to guide ships sailing on the Mediterranean Sea and the Nile River into Alexandria's harbor. Look carefully at this photograph. See, here I am at the top part of the lighthouse."

Kelly looked at the photograph. She saw her sister by a fire inside an open, domelike structure.

"They had to use a fire for their light source," Anna explained. "Behind the fire, at the back of the dome, is a large, curved mirror made of polished bronze. The mirror was used to project the fire's light into a beam. The lighthouse keeper told me that ships could detect the light from the tower at night or the smoke from the fire during the day up to 100 miles away."

"The lighthouse keeper also told me why there was a 600-foot spiral ramp in the building. It was so animals could pull carts filled with materials to the top! He also showed me the shaft with the dumbwaiter that was used to transport fuel up to the fire. Most likely, the lighthouse was 140 meters high, and at that time, it was one of the tallest structures in the world. Can you imagine such a tall, slim, single column of that height? It was beautiful, but it was practical, too. No wonder its design became the basis for all our lighthouses today."

"I know from your description that you weren't at the Great Lighthouse of Alexandria," Kelly told Anna, "but if you admit to making up your story, I'll take you for a real visit to it."

"There can't be one iota of truth to that," scoffed Anna. "It isn't possible for you to take me to see any of the Seven Wonders of the Ancient World. I told you already that none of them is in existence today. The lighthouse was destroyed in 1303 AD by a huge earthquake."

"Oh, there's more than an iota of truth to what I said," Kelly said with a broad smile. "I can take you to see the lighthouse. All we have to do is put on scuba gear. Archaeologists discovered the remains of the lighthouse in the 1990s, and now you can go diving and see the ruins on the floor of Alexandria's harbor."

How did Kelly know that Anna was making up her story? It is time to check facts.

Dictionary

1. What is the meaning of *iota*? _____

   _____

2. Is there one iota of truth to this sentence: *The ninth letter of the Greek alphabet is iota?* Explain your answer in a sentence.

   _____

   _____

Metric Converter

1. Height of outside of lighthouse: _____ feet = 140 meters

2. Length of spiral ramp inside lighthouse: 600 feet = _____ meters

3. Was the ramp longer than the lighthouse was high?   **Yes**   **No**

Image Search

List two ways the image of the Lighthouse of Alexandria differs from Anna's description of "a tall, slim, single column."

1. _____

2. _____

Search Engine/Encyclopedia

1. Is the Lighthouse of Alexandria one of the Seven Wonders of the Ancient World?   **Yes**   **No**

2. Which one, if any, of the Seven Wonders of the Ancient World is not in ruins and is still in existence today?

   _____

In Your Own Words

People have put together new lists of Seven Wonders. Some of these lists include natural and engineering wonders of the modern world. Think of one place and one structure you might put on these lists. On a separate piece of paper, write a paragraph in which you describe the structure and the place. Tell why you think they merit being on a list of Seven Wonders.

Losing on Purpose

"My Olympic hero lost his race on purpose." When Matt said that, the rest of the class burst out laughing. The teacher Mr. Baker had to ask everyone to be quiet while Matt finished his report.

"His name is Lawrence Lemieux," Matt continued. "Lemieux was participating in the 1988 Seoul Olympics. Seoul is the capital of China. Lemieux was born in a capital city, too, but he was born in Edmonton. Edmonton is the capital of Canada. Lemieux was in the solo sailing race. Even though the seas were exceptionally rough, Lemieux had sailed at a fast clip. Conditions became hazardous when the winds escalated from 15 to 35 knots, but halfway through the race, Lemieux still had a firm grip on the silver medal. Then disaster struck."

Matt paused before saying, "Lemieux heard the cries of two sailors from Singapore. Singapore is the capital of Taiwan. The sailors were competing in a different but nearby event. Their boat had capsized under the waves in the rough seas. Both crewmembers were injured. One of the sailors was clinging desperately to the boat's hull. The other was 50 feet away and being swept off by the currents.

"Lemieux immediately turned his boat and made his way to the sailor that was drifting away. Lemieux had to lift him onto his own boat because the sailor was too badly hurt to climb aboard himself. Next, Lemieux sailed over to the capsized craft and rescued the sailor who was desperately clinging to its hull. Then Lemieux turned his boat against the wind and held it steady until a rescue boat arrived. After the injured sailors were picked up by the rescue boat, Lemieux could have quit. Instead, he **resumed** racing! He resumed racing even though he could no longer win a medal."

Matt concluded, "Lemieux is my hero because he embodies the true Olympic spirit. He showed courage and bravery, and when he resumed the race, he showed he was a true competitor."

"Lemieux is indeed a hero," Courtney said, "but are you sure this happened in the Olympics? I don't think they have sailing races. Aren't the summer Olympics just track-and-field events?"

Matt answered, "Sailing events were scheduled for the 1896 Olympic Games in Athens. Athens is the capital of Greece. Those events were cancelled though due to severe weather. Since then, there have been sailing events in every Olympics except the 1904 games. Those games were held in St. Louis. St. Louis is not the capital of a country, but it is the capital of a state. St. Louis is the capital of Missouri."

Mr. Baker said, "I think we should all give a hand to Matt. He has taught us quite a few things about the Olympics." After everyone had applauded, Mr. Baker said, "We will resume our hero reports tomorrow, but now it is time for a review on capital cities."

Losing on Purpose *(cont.)*

What capital cities need to be reviewed? It is time to check facts.

Thesaurus

1. Which word is a synonym for *resume*?

Ⓐ sail   Ⓑ restart   Ⓒ conclude   Ⓓ hull

2. Is there any activity or sport that you stopped playing or doing for a while and would like to *resume*? Answer in one or two sentences.

_____

_____

Search Engine/Encyclopedia

For questions #1–4, write **True** or **False**. If your answer is **False**, cross out the incorrect word(s) and write the correct word(s) on the line.

_____ **1.** Seoul is the capital of China. _____

_____ **2.** Edmonton is the capital of Canada. _____

_____ **3.** Athens is the capital of Greece. _____

_____ **4.** St. Louis is the capital of Missouri. _____

5. List two other summer Olympic events that are not in track or field.

_____   _____

Calculator

> 1 knot = 1.151 miles per hour (mph)
>
> 1 knot = 1.852 kilometers per hour (kmph)

1. 15–35 knots = _____ to _____ mph

2. 15–35 knots = _____ to _____ kmph

In Your Own Words

On a separate piece of paper, write a paragraph in which you tell why one can be a hero without winning. Use information from the story in your answer. You can use information about another person, too, if you want.

"What's the rarest animal you've ever seen?" Aliya asked.

"The rarest animal I've ever seen is the dodo," answered Kevin. "The dodo is from the island of Mauritius, but I saw it in the zoo."

"Are you sure you saw a dodo from Mauritius?" asked Aliya.

"Yes, I'm sure," Kevin said with certainty. "The dodo is a large, flightless bird that is about one meter tall and weighs 10 to 18 kilograms. I know the dodo comes from Mauritius because it is an **endemic** species. It doesn't live anywhere else in the world, only in Mauritius. Mauritius is a tropical island situated by the Tropic of Cancer. It is off the southeast coast of the African continent in the Atlantic Ocean, east of Madagascar. There are only two seasons in Mauritius. One season has a mean temperature of 24.7° Celsius. The other season has a mean temperature of 20.4° Celsius. Sea temperature in the lagoon around Mauritius varies from 71.6° Fahrenheit to 80.6° Fahrenheit."

"I saw an endemic species, too," Lucy said. "The animal I saw was endemic to Australia, Tasmania, and New Guinea. It is the Tasmanian tiger. I saw this species when my family went to Tasmania. Tasmania is an Australian island and state. The Tasmanian tiger is the largest carnivorous marsupial. Carnivores eat meat. Marsupials have pouches. So that means the Tasmanian tiger eats meat and carries its young in a pouch."

Kento said, "I saw the Western Black Rhinoceros at the zoo. This particular rhino is a subspecies of the Black Rhinoceros. This subspecies wasn't endemic to just one country. It was once widespread in central West Africa. It lived in the savannah, browsing on the grass. Today, though, it's really rare. People are trying to protect it, but these animals are being killed by poachers for their horns. Did you know that these rhinos have two horns? And do you know what rhino horns have in common with hair, fingernails, and animal hooves? They are all mostly made up of keratin. Keratin is a tough protein."

Aliya said, "I'm not sure the three of you saw what you think you saw."

"Why don't you believe us?" asked Kevin. "Don't you think there are large, flightless birds?"

"Don't you think there are marsupials that eat meat?" asked Lucy.

"Is it so hard to believe that hair, fingernails, and rhino horns are all made up of keratin?" asked Kento.

Aliya laughed and said, "I know there were dodos. I know there were Tasmanian tigers. I know there were Western Black rhinos. The question you should be asking me is, 'Are these animals extinct?'"

Could these rare animals have been seen at these locations? It is time to check facts.

Dictionary

What is the meaning of *endemic*? _____

_____

Atlas

Write **True** or **False**. If your answer is **False**, cross out the incorrect word(s) and write the correct word(s) on the line.

_____ **1.** Mauritius is situated by the Tropic of Cancer. _____

_____ **2.** Mauritius is off the southeast coast of Africa. _____

_____ **3.** Mauritius is in the Atlantic Ocean. _____

_____ **4.** Mauritius is east of Madagascar. _____

Temperature Converter

1. Air around Mauritius: 20.4°C to 24.7°C = _____°F to _____ °F

2. Water around Mauritius: _____°C to _____°C = 71.6°F to 80.6°F

3. Can the water be warmer than the air?   **Yes**   **No**

Image Search

Key Words: 🔍 *dodo*   🔍 *Tasmanian tiger*   🔍 *Western Black Rhinooceros*

1. Which animal has stripes? _____

2. Does the dodo have horns? _____

Search Engine/Encyclopedia

1. Are hair, fingernails, and rhino horns made of keratin?   **Yes**   **No**

2. Put a check by the animals that are extinct.

_____ dodo _____ Tasmanian tiger _____ Western Black Rhinoceros

In Your Own Words

Think like a debater. On a separate piece of paper, write a paragraph in which you say why we should work to stop animals from becoming extinct. Give at least two reasons. Then write a second paragraph in which you give two reasons why we should not.

Douglas and Gwendalyn went to the Botanical Gardens. Gwendalyn wanted to first go inside the conservatory. "It's an amazing greenhouse," Gwendalyn said, "with a special desert wing filled with **hardy** cacti, as well as a tropical wing filled with orchids."

In one of the outside gardens, Douglas saw a gnarled and stunted-looking tree he didn't recognize. It had green pine needles that covered its twisted branches and, unlike the other trees and plants, it was not marked with a sign. Gwendalyn noticed a man and a woman just a bit down the path who were digging up plants and putting them in a small wagon. "Let's ask those workers over there what it is," Gwendalyn said.

When Gwendolyn asked, the male worker said, "Oh, that tree is a Bristlecone pine. Bristlecone pines are a hardy species that can live to be 5,000 years old."

"I don't think trees can grow that long," Gwendalyn said.

"This species can," the female worker said quickly. "You're just unfamiliar with Bristlecone pines because they usually live where it's really cold. The cold and the short growing season is in part why they grow so slowly. There are only a few small groves left in Antarctica."

"You must learn a lot about plants working here," Douglas said. "What are you digging up? Are you going to transplant those plants somewhere?"

The man said, "Oh, these plants are a common, hardy species that can grow anywhere. We're just clearing them out so we can plant some banana trees here."

"Banana trees!" exclaimed Gwendalyn. "Are bananas a hardy species, too?"

"No, they're easy to grow," answered the woman. "Here, I'll give you some of our seeds if you go away and let us get back to work." The woman handed Gwendalyn a handful of seeds. Each seed was about the size of a peanut.

"I didn't know seeds could be this big," Gwendalyn said.

"This banana seed is tiny compared to the biggest seed," the man said to Gwendalyn. "The biggest seed is from the Coco de Mer palm that grows in the Seychelles. That palm tree once had a fruit that weighed 42 kilograms and a seed that weighed 17.6 kilograms."

The woman worker said, "Don't tell anyone in the conservatory that we gave you banana tree seeds. Now please let us get back to work."

When Douglas and Gwendalyn entered the conservatory, Douglas said, "Before we visit the desert and tropical wings, we have to find someone in authority to tell them about those people."

"But they asked us not to," Gwendalyn said.

Douglas said, "They asked us not to because they don't work here. They were thieves who were digging up and stealing plants."

What does Douglas know that Gwendalyn doesn't? It is time to check facts.

Thesaurus

1. Write down two synonyms for *hardy*.

_____   _____

2. An antonym for *hardy* might be

Ⓐ weak.   Ⓑ biggest.   Ⓒ exterior.   Ⓓ tropical.

3. Name a job that you would need to be hardy to do. Explain.

_____

_____

Image Search

Key Words: 🔍 *bristlecone pine tree*   🔍 *Coco de Mar palm seed*

1. Do Bristlecone pines have twisted branches?   **Yes   No**

2. Is the Coco de Mer palm seed red?   **Yes   No**

Metric Converter

Convert the Coco de Mer's records into pounds.

1. Fruit: 42 kilograms = _____ pounds

2. Seed: 17.6 kilograms = _____ pounds

Search Engine/Encyclopedia

1. Where do Bristlecone pine trees live? _____

2. Can Bristlecone pines live to 5,000 years?   **Yes   No**

3. Do bananas have seeds the size of peanuts?   **Yes   No**

In Your Own Words

On a separate piece of paper, write a paragraph in which you explain why Douglas feels that the man and the woman digging up the plants were thieves rather than workers for the botanical garden.

The Junior Rangers had come to a stream. Should they cross or not cross? In the past three days, the Junior Rangers had hiked 32 miles on rugged trails into the back country of Mount Rainier National Park. They were completely on their own. If one of them slipped and was swept away while fording the stream, there was no one to help them.

Ranger Loy looked at the six Junior Rangers he was training and chose Gary. "Why don't you tell us everything we're supposed to know about crossing streams safely?" he asked. The remaining Junior Rangers were pleased that Gary had been asked. Gary was known for being **verbose**. If Gary used a lot of words, it meant more time for the other Junior Rangers to rest!

Gary started with a rush of words. "As you know, Mount Rainier is a volcano in the Rocky Mountains with a summit elevation of 14,411 feet. That makes it the highest mountain in the state of Washington. It is located just 54 miles southeast of Seattle. Many people think Seattle is the capital of Washington, but it isn't."

"Try not to be so verbose, Gary," Ranger Loy cut in gently. "Only give us the necessary precautions for fording streams."

Laughing, Gary said, "Okay, I'll try to stick to the topic, use fewer words, and not be so verbose. As you well know, many hikers underestimate the power of moving water. No matter how many streams you have already crossed, you must always assess the current situation to cross a stream safely. Ideally, you want to cross in the early morning because that is when water levels are lowest. You also want to cross in an area with a smooth bottom and slow-moving water that is below knee height. To check the water level, you can use a stick. You can also use a stick to see if the water is moving too fast by simply dropping the stick into the water and walking alongside it. If you can't keep up with the stick, the water is flowing too fast for you to safely ford the stream.

"Now remember," Gary cautioned, "you must also scout downstream before settling on your crossing site. If you spot log jams, waterfalls, or other hazards that could trap you, you want to choose an alternate site. You should also find potential sites you could climb out at if you do fall in.

"When fording the stream, you should use a sturdy stick to maintain two points of contact with the ground at all times as you cross, and you should look forward as much as possible because staring down at moving water can make you dizzy. Before you cross, you should unfasten the belt of your pack. That way, if you do fall in and it becomes necessary for you to discard your pack, it will be easier to slip out of it. In addition, if you do fall in, you should try to keep your feet pointing downstream and your head up."

"Enough!" Ranger Loy said with a smile. "Gary, despite your verboseness and one incorrect piece of information, you covered some important precautions."

What was Gary's one incorrect piece of information? It is time to check facts.

Dictionary

1. What is the meaning of *verbose*? _____

2. Which response is the least verbose?

   Ⓐ I'm sinking, so please come to my aid.

   Ⓑ Oh, dear, water is coming in so I need help.

   Ⓒ Boat flooding. Help!

   Ⓓ I think perhaps you should come help us.

Metric Converter

1. How far did the Junior Rangers walk? 32 miles = _____ kilometers

2. What is Mount Rainier's summit elevation? 14,411 feet = _____ meters

Image Search

Can you tell from pictures if Mt. Rainier is a volcano? Explain your answer.

_____

_____

Atlas

Look at a map of Washington to find the correct answers.

1. Is Mount Rainier southeast of Seattle?   **Yes**   **No**

2. What is the capital of Washington? _____

Search Engine/Encyclopedia

Write **True** or **False**. If your answer is **False**, cross out the incorrect word(s) and write the correct word(s) on the line.

_____ 1. Mount Rainier a volcano. _____

_____ 2. Mount Rainier is in the Rocky Mountains. _____

In Your Own Words

On a separate piece of paper, write down some of Gary's precautions (which were all true!) for crossing a stream safely. Do this in a less verbose way by making a numbered list. Write a title for your list of instructions, too.

Magellan's Diary

I may have found some pages from Ferdinand Magellan's diary," Alex told his friend Cassie.

"Do you mean the famous Portuguese explorer Ferdinand Magellan?" Cassie asked doubtfully.

"That's the man!" exclaimed Alex. "I found these pages stuck in an antique seaman's chest. Here, read them and tell me what you think." Alex carefully handed Cassie some old and fragile-looking pieces of paper. Cassie had to focus carefully on the scratchy writing because the ink had faded and turned brown.

April 1542

It is now 20 years since I have returned safely from my trip around the world. On that expedition, we were the first to sail from the Atlantic Ocean into the Pacific Ocean. On that day, we encountered favorable winds, and that is why I named the world's largest ocean Mar Pacifico. We were also the first expedition to circumnavigate the Earth. Now that I am old, people ask me what I am most proud of.

I am proud of three things. I am proud that they named the strait we sailed through at the bottom of Africa the Strait of Magellan. I am proud that I was the first to successfully sail around the globe. I am most proud of leaving with five ships and 237 men and arriving back home after three years without the loss of a single man. Eu não falo a verdade.

Cassie looked up from the pages Alex had handed her. She said, "I know that the Pacific Ocean was named by Magellan. He called it the Pacific because it was pacific when he sailed on it. I wonder what he would have named it if he hadn't been so pacific at that time. Just think, if Magellan's ships had been beset by hurricanes and huge waves, Magellan might have called the ocean Mar Feroz instead of Mar Pacifico."

"If Magellan did name the Pacific, then maybe this is a genuine entry," Alex cried in excitement. Alex was so happy at the thought of his discovery that he began to jump up and down.

Cassie laughed at Alex's exuberance and said, "Even if the words in Portuguese at the end swear that what is written is the truth, the diary cannot be Magellan's."

"What do you mean?" asked Alex as he stopped jumping in excitement. "How can you be so **pacific** when what you are telling me is such a disappointment to me? Don't you want to scream and cry in anger and fury?"

"No," laughed Cassie. "I knew it couldn't be real when I read the date and the very first line."

"But the year 1542 is 20 years after Magellan's expedition successfully completed circumnavigating the Earth," Alex protested.

Does Cassie know something that Alex doesn't? It is time to check facts.

Thesaurus

1. Write down two synonyms and two antonyms for *pacific*.

   synonyms: _____   _____

   antonyms: _____   _____

2. You want to make a pacific gesture when you greet someone. Do you show an open palm or a fist? _____

Translator (from Portuguese to English)

1. *Mar Feroz* _____

2. *Eu não falo a verdade.* _____

Atlas

The Strait of Magellan is

- Ⓐ close to the tip of Africa.
- Ⓑ close to the tip of South America.
- Ⓒ between the Indian and Pacific Ocean.
- Ⓓ between the Atlantic Ocean and the Mediterranean Sea.

Search Engine/Encyclopedia

Look at these five statements. Two are false. Circle them.

- Magellan circumnavigated the globe between 1519–1522.
- Magellan left with 5 ships and 237 men.
- Magellan sailed by New Zealand.
- Magellan was the first to sail from the Atlantic to the Pacific Ocean.
- Magellan, all five ships, and all his men arrived safely home.

In Your Own Words

Would you have wanted to be one of Magellan's crew members on this expedition? On a separate piece of paper, write a paragraph in which you tell why or why not. In your paragraph, provide a few facts about the expedition (where it went and time period). Remember, there is no right or wrong answer. It is your personal choice.

Invasion from Mars

"Martians were invading from Mars! It was broadcast on the radio," Sarah told Lily. "The broadcast terrified many people and caused them to panic."

"I don't believe it," Lily said. "It is **unfathomable** that anyone would believe such a thing."

"The broadcast made it seem more than fathomable. It was easy to believe because the broadcast made it appear as if the invasion was happening right at that very moment. The broadcast was actually a play that was adapted from a novel by H.G. Wells called *The War of the Worlds*. The play was cleverly written. Parts of the play sounded like interruptions of breaking news. The breaking news interruptions got more frequent and terrifying as the play went on.

"First, you hear about a cylindrical meteorite that lands in Grover's Mill, New Jersey. Then you hear about the meteorite unscrewing and a Martian with tentacles coming out. The Martian incinerates the crowd with heat rays. Shouts are cut off in mid-sentence. Later you hear about destroyed power stations, huge gas explosions, and refugees clogging roads. You even hear a voice that sounded like the president's.

"One especially terrifying part of the broadcast has a part in which a news reporter sounds as if he is broadcasting on top of a building in New York City. He describes five great machines of unfathomable power and evil. The machines emit poison smoke that drifts over the city. You hear about people running and diving into the East River 'like rats' and 'falling like flies.' Finally, the broadcaster himself is done in by the poison smoke."

Lily was silent for a moment. Then she said, "I just find it unfathomable that anyone would believe it. When did this happen?"

Sarah answered, "The broadcast was aired on October 30, 1938. It was directed and narrated by a man named Orson Welles. Welles was the man who directed the radio actor to sound like President Franklin D. Roosevelt."

"But how could anyone believe this was actually happening? I have a hard time believing there is even an author named H.G. Wells who wrote such a book. I'm also sure that Franklin D. Roosevelt wasn't president at that time. Furthermore, if the Martians had landed in New Jersey, it is unfathomable that they could get to New York City during the time of the broadcast. The distance is too far. I'm sorry, but I just don't believe a broadcast like this every happened."

"Fictional Martians can do anything," laughed Sarah, "but it's only about 55 miles from Grover's Mill, New Jersey, to New York City. This broadcast truly aired. The people that mostly panicked were the ones that only heard part of the broadcast. The broadcast actually ends like the book."

"How did the book end?" asked Lily curiously.

"Oh, the Martians don't have any immunity to the germs on Earth, so they all die."

"So, germs are the good guys?" laughed Lily. "This story gets worse every minute."

Should Lily believe all of what Sarah said? It is time to check facts.

Dictionary

1. What is the meaning of *unfathomable*? _____

2. Hundreds of years ago, people did not know about germs. Why do you think it was unfathomable then but fathomable now?

_____

_____

Search Engine/Encyclopedia

Write **True** or **False**. If your answer is **False**, rewrite the sentence so it's true.

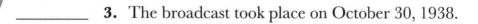

_____ **1.** H.G. Wells wrote a book called *The War of the Worlds*.

_____

_____ **2.** Orson Welles narrated a radio broadcast of *The War of the Worlds*.

_____

_____ **3.** The broadcast took place on October 30, 1938.

_____

_____ **4.** Some people believed Martians were invading.

_____

_____ **5.** Franklin Roosevelt was president in 1938.

_____

Atlas

A = Grover Mill Road, Lawrence Township, NJ

B = New York City, NY

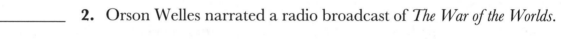

About how many miles is it from A to B? _____

In Your Own Words

How do you decide if something you hear on the radio or see on television is truthful or not? Do you think you could be tricked? On a separate piece of paper, write a paragraph in which you explain. If you can, use an example from your own life.

Would You Hire this Person?

Dr. Orion needed to hire someone to help develop programs for the planetarium. Charles was first on the interview list. "On paper, this man seems like a **stellar** candidate," Dr. Orion thought to himself as he buzzed Charles in.

Dr. Orion smiled at Charles. "Your resume is very impressive," he said as Charles sat down. "You sound very knowledgeable, but to us, a stellar candidate will be more than knowledgeable. He or she will need to be creative and imaginative, too. That way, he or she can develop programs that will interest people and make them want to come to the planetarium. So, how did you first get interested in planets, stars, and other celestial objects?"

"I wish I could say it was by going to a planetarium and seeing a show," laughed Charles, "but the truth is that it was my state flag. You see, I'm from the state of South Carolina. South Carolina's state flag is a field of blue emblazoned with the eight gold stars that make up the Big Dipper. The state flag made me want to locate the Big Dipper in the sky. Every night when I went to bed, I looked at the Big Dipper out my bedroom window. It was a great comfort to me that it was always in the exact same location every night of the year no matter what time I went to bed or even if I woke up in the middle of the night."

"You saw the Big Dipper in the same location at all hours every night?" asked Dr. Orion.

Charles laughed and replied, "Of course I couldn't see it every night. Sometimes it was cloudy, but even on some cloudy nights, I could spot it because of Polaris."

"Do you mean the North Star?" asked Dr. Orion.

"Yes, Polaris," answered Charles. "The star that is easiest to find because it is the brightest in the sky. It's the star that is almost straight above Earth's North Pole. All the other stars look like they move in a circle in the sky because of the Earth's rotation, but Polaris seems to stay still because of its location. That's why sailors have used it to navigate for centuries. Did you know that Polaris wasn't always the North Star? Polaris became the North Star in about AD 500. Before, the North Star was a star called Thuban. Thuban is in the Draco constellation, but Polaris is in the Ursa Major constellation."

Charles smiled widely and continued, "If you hire me, I know I would do a stellar job. I'd create programs that are interesting and informative. I've already got an idea for a program on the constellations. I'd show where the constellations are located and tell how they got their names. Did you know that a lot of constellation names are Latin? Draco and Ursa Major, of course, are Latin words, but so are Aries, Cancer, Cygnus, Pisces, Scorpius, Leo, and Canis Major."

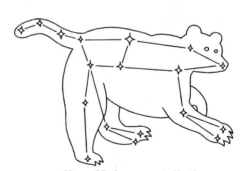

Ursa Major constellation

When the interview was over, Dr. Orion shook Charles's hand. "We will be notifying you in a few days concerning our decision," he said. "Thank you for coming."

Would You Hire this Person? *(cont.)*

Should Dr. Orion hire Charles? It is time to check facts.

Dictionary

1. Give two meanings for the word *stellar*. _____ _____

2. Fill in the blanks: I think . . .

   _____ is a stellar actor.

   _____ is a stellar singer.

   _____ is a stellar athlete.

Image Search

Describe in a few words the state flag of these states.

1. South Carolina _____

2. Alaska _____

Search Engine/Encyclopedia

Write **True** or **False**. If your answer is **False**, cross out the incorrect word(s) and write the correct word(s) on the line.

_____ 1. The Big Dipper is made up of eight stars. _____

_____ 2. Polaris is part of the Big Dipper. _____

_____ 3. The North Star is the same as Polaris. _____

_____ 4. The North Star has not always been Polaris. _____

_____ 5. Polaris is in the Ursa Major constellation. _____

Translator *(from Latin to English)*

1. Draco _____
2. Ursa Major _____
3. Aries _____
4. Cancer _____
5. Pisces _____
6. Scorpius _____
7. Leo _____
8. Cygnus _____

In Your Own Words

On a separate piece of paper, write one or two paragraphs in which you explain why or why not Dr. Orion should hire Charles. Use specific examples from the story.

Elephant Dictionary

"I know someone who has walked 33,000 kilometers to work," Lina said to Tara. "That's over 20,000 miles!"

"Is this another one of your wild stories?" asked Tara.

Lina laughed and said, "No, this story is the absolute truth. The woman's name is Andrea Turkalo. For the past 20 years, Turkalo has walked back and forth every day on a trail in a very **remote** part of the world."

"I'm still skeptical," Tara said, "but do tell me where this trail is."

"This remote trail is deep in a tropical forest in the Central African Republic," Lina answered. "The Central Africa Republic is south of Cameroon and north of Chad. The trail cuts through huge, ancient trees. It ends in a clearing with the name Dzanga Bai. Turkalo sits in an open shelter every day and looks out at the clearing. Do you have any idea why?"

"I don't have the remotest idea," answered Tara, "but I am sure you will tell me."

"Turkalo is watching forest elephants! Every day, forest elephants come to drink from the mineral springs in the clearing to get salt and other minerals needed in their diet. The elephants hang out there, and sometimes there are 100 or more. Turkalo can recognize over 600. She knows everything about them. She is helping to make an elephant dictionary."

Tara started to laugh. She said, "I was skeptical before of a few things you said. Now I am no longer skeptical. Now I know you are making this up because elephants don't have a language!"

Lina protested, "Elephants do, too! It ends up that elephants often communicate using sounds below the threshold of human hearing. These sounds carry over vast distances. Believe it or not, elephants use specific sounds to communicate to other elephants and maintain family ties. Elephants can talk to each other even when they are 10 kilometers, or 6.2 miles, apart."

Lina explained further. "It was a scientist named Katy Payne who first figured this out. Payne was studying whales and recording their songs with special equipment. Humans can't hear whale songs, either. Then Payne went to the zoo in Portland."

"There's a Portland in Central African Republic?" interrupted Tara.

"Of course not," Lina said. Portland is the capital of the state of Oregon. That's where Payne was when she saw two Asian elephants that were standing on opposite sides of a concrete wall. Payne felt a throbbing in her ears and in the air, and this made her wonder if, like whales, elephants could communicate at a pitch below what humans could hear. Special recording equipment proved that Payne was right."

Tara was silent for a moment. Then she said, "Even if you are right about an elephant dictionary, you still don't have all your facts straight."

What is it that Lina said that Tara doesn't agree with? It is time to check facts.

Thesaurus

1. Write down three synonyms for *remote*.

_____ _____ _____

2. What word is not an antonym for *remote*?

Ⓐ convenient Ⓑ close Ⓒ pretty Ⓓ possible

Calculator

If Andrea walked about 20,000 miles in 20 years, how far did she walk each day?

1.   _____20_____   x   _____365_____   =   _____
number of years *number of days in a year* *number of total days*

2.   ___20,000___   ÷   _____   =   _____
total miles *answer from #1* *number of miles per day*

Image Search

Key Words: 🔍 *Dzanga Bai*

Why might it be easier to study elephants here rather than in the forest?

_____

Atlas

1. What direction is Cameroon to the Central African Republic? _____

2. What direction is Chad to the Central African Republic? _____

3. Is your answer in agreement to what Lina said?   **Yes**   **No**

Search Engine/Encyclopedia

1. What is the capital of Oregon? _____

2. Is Andrea Turkalo a real person who studies elephants?   **Yes**   **No**

3. Is Katy Payne a real person who studied elephants?   **Yes**   **No**

In Your Own Words

Imagine you are making an elephant dictionary. How would you go about it? How would you decide what a word means? How could you test it? Use a separate piece of paper to explain your elephant dictionary.

As Molly and Jake ambled leisurely down the street, they passed a store that specialized in maps. Molly said, "Oh, let's go in and look around. I think cartography is amazing. Maybe I can find a colorful map of Central America. I have to memorize all the countries in Central America for school. If I hang up a map of that area in the kitchen, I can look at it every time I eat to familiarize myself with the region."

As they entered, Jake cautioned Molly. "Remember," he said, "you are always making **rash** purchases. If you do buy a map, don't be imprudent. Think carefully before you pay for it. Make sure it really is a map you like and can use."

"Don't worry," Molly assured Jake. "I won't make any rash or imprudent decisions because I won't purchase anything without your approval." It wasn't soon after she said these words that Molly held up a map for Jake to see. "Look at this one!" she cried in delight. "It was printed in 1850, but it still has the ten countries that make up Central America. It even has the Panama Canal."

"The Panama Canal is one of the most amazing structures made by modern man," Jake said. "It is an 82-kilometer, or 16-mile, strip that connects the Atlantic Ocean via the Caribbean Sea to the Pacific Ocean. The canal is a key conduit for international maritime trade. Instead of sailing the lengthy route around the southernmost tip of South America, ships can just cut across the Isthmus of Panama. This shortcut allows them to make the trip in half the time. Did you know that when the canal first opened, about 1,000 ships went through in a year? In 2008, the annual number rose to over 14,700! That means the number of ships has gone from one a day to about 20 a day, and every year it's getting higher."

Jake looked carefully at the map Molly held up. After a moment, he said, "Molly, buying this map would be a rash and imprudent thing to do. You shouldn't buy it."

"What do you mean?" demanded Molly. "Every North American country that fits into the subcategory of Central America is there. Mexico isn't because it's not considered part of Central America, but Guatemala is. So are Belize, El Salvador, Honduras, and Nicaragua. There's Costa Rica, too, and Angola, Columbia, Ecuador. Finally, there's the southernmost country— Panama."

Jake cautioned, "Molly, don't be rash and buy the map. It really would be imprudent."

"What do I need to think about?" asked Molly. "This map is fine."

"Think about when the Panama Canal was constructed," answered Jake.

Molly was silent for a moment as she looked at the map. "You know," she said slowly, "I think we both need to check things. You need to check your math, and I need to check on the number of countries in Central America."

Do both Jake and Molly need to check on some things? It is time to check facts.

Thesaurus

1. List two synonyms for *rash* that fit the way it was used in this story.

_____   _____

2. Describe a time when you or someone you know made a rash decision.

_____

_____

Metric Converter

The Panama Canal is 82 kilometers. Now check Jake's conversions.

1. 82 kilometers = _____ miles

2. Was Jake right when he said that it equaled 16 miles?   **Yes**   **No**

Calculator

Jake's total ship numbers were correct when he gave the entire year amount (1,000 in the first year, and 14,700 in 2008). Now check his math.

1. 1,000 ÷ 365 = _____

2. 14,700 ÷ 365 = _____

3. Was he right about about how many boats per day went through the canal?   **Yes**   **No**

Search Engine/Encyclopedia

1. During which years was the Panama Canal constructed?

Ⓐ 1776–1782   Ⓑ 1843–1852   Ⓒ 1881–1914   Ⓓ 1961–1971

2. List the countries in Central America. _____

_____

In Your Own Words

If someone in Central America was describing where they lived, they could say they lived both in Central America and North America. On a separate piece of paper, describe the location of your home. Go from small to big starting with your street address and ending with the Milky Way Galaxy. Mention hemispheres in your answer.

Jacques and Hillary were walking down the street when they passed a flower shop. Jacques said, "Let's go in. My grandmother Bernadette has been ill, and I would like to send her some flowers."

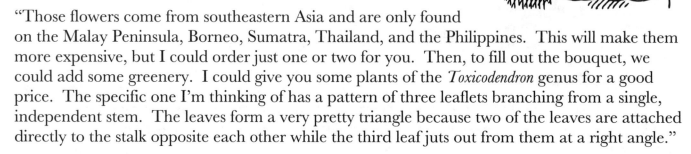

"You should send roses because roses are beautiful, elegant, and very **aromatic**," the florist told Jacques. "Other flowers may be as colorful, but few are as aromatic as the rose."

"Roses do have a nice aroma," Hillary agreed. "I have always liked the way they smell."

Jacques said, "There must be other aromatic flowers. I know! Have you heard of the rafflesia flower? I don't know much about them, but I've heard that they are very aromatic. Do you have any in the shop?"

"Those flowers come from southeastern Asia and are only found on the Malay Peninsula, Borneo, Sumatra, Thailand, and the Philippines. This will make them more expensive, but I could order just one or two for you. Then, to fill out the bouquet, we could add some greenery. I could give you some plants of the *Toxicodendron* genus for a good price. The specific one I'm thinking of has a pattern of three leaflets branching from a single, independent stem. The leaves form a very pretty triangle because two of the leaves are attached directly to the stalk opposite each other while the third leaf juts out from them at a right angle."

"Do you think that will be enough?" asked Jacques doubtfully.

"Well," said the florist thoughtfully, "we can arrange the flowers in a basket with some fruit. We can add red, green, pink, and yellow apples for a decorative touch."

"Fruit is a good idea!" Jacques said, "but apples don't seem that special. Do you know anything about the durian fruit? I don't know much about them, but I've heard they are very aromatic."

The florist said, "Of course, I have heard of them. The durian is a strictly tropical fruit. Did you know that it stops growing when the mean daily temperature drops below 22 degrees Celsius? The good thing about it is that it's from Southeast Asia, too. This means I can order the rafflesia and the durian from the same company. I think I'll order you half a dozen durians. If that's agreeable to you, I can place the order as soon as you pay."

Jacques wrote on a card in French, "*Vous sentez aussi bon que ces fleurs,*" and then began to take out his wallet. He stopped when Hillary put a hand on his arm and said, "Jacques, this bouquet will be aromatic, but I don't think you want to send it to your grandmother."

"Why ever not?" questioned Jacques. "I think it sounds like a perfect fruit-and-flower arrangement."

What does Hillary know that Jacques doesn't? It is time to check facts.

Dictionary

1. If something is aromatic, it _____

2. Which place is most likely the most aromatic?

   Ⓐ bakery   Ⓑ library   Ⓒ book store   Ⓓ shoe store

Atlas

Put a checkmark (✓) next to the countries and places that are in Southeastern Asia:

_____ Malay Peninsula   _____ Thailand

_____ Borneo   _____ Philippines

_____ Sumatra

Temperature Converter

The durian fruit stops growing when the temperature drops below 22°C.

   22°C = _____ °F

Search Engine/Encyclopedia

1. Describe the rafflesia's aroma and size in a few words. _____
   _____

2. Name a plant that belongs to the genus *Toxicodendron*. _____

3. Describe the durian's appearance and smell in a few words. _____
   _____

Translator (from French to English)

Vous sentez aussi bon que ces fleurs! _____

In Your Own Words

On a separate piece of paper, write a paragraph in which you explain why Jacques might not want to send the floral arrangement he is thinking of ordering to his grandmother. Then describe one you would choose if you were going to send one.

Mineola and Odakato were at a Plains Indians exhibition and festival. There were dancers, singers, and exhibits, as well as information and activity booths. There were **vendors**, too. The vendors were selling food, crafts, and other items.

The two friends went into a booth that was selling traditional items made out of animal hides. Picking up a medium-sized, painted drum, Mineola said, "This would make a good gift for my grandfather. I wonder how much it costs."

When Mineola found out the price, she gasped. "How can this drum be so expensive?" she asked. "What makes it so special?"

The merchant answered, "The question to ask is not why this drum is so expensive but why is it worth so much. First, it came from the Four Corners area. Second, it is handmade from a buffalo hide and very old. This is not a cheap, modern-day replica. Third, look at the paintings on it. They are masterful and filled with intricate and precise details. This drum probably should be in a museum, but I got it from a man who was moving to Australia and who was in a hurry to sell most of his possessions so he wouldn't have to pay to have them shipped or stored."

As Mineola studied the drum, she asked, "What is the Four Corners area?"

"Oh," said the vendor, "the Four Corners is a region of the United States. It's named after the quadripoint where the boundaries of four states meet."

"So you can stand in Wyoming, South Dakota, Nebraska, and Colorado at the same time?" asked Odakato.

"Right!" answered the merchant. "The people who lived there were well known for their buffalo-hide paintings. This drum was most likely painted by a man because men painted living things while the women traditionally painted abstract and geometric designs. The painting on the drum depicts a battle with warriors and horses. If you turn the drum from right to left, you can follow the course of the battle. At the end, you can see the victors leading all the captured horses away."

"How old did you say this drum was?" Mineola asked the merchant.

"Ah," the vendor smiled at Mineola, "the age of this drum makes it an antiquity. This drum is easily over 600 years old."

"I can see why this drum is worth so much," Mineola said, as she carefully turned it over and studied the paintings. "Still, I can't afford your price of 500 U.S. dollars."

"How much do you have?" asked the vendor. "If this is truly for your grandfather, perhaps I can give you a special deal."

Odakato cut in. He said, "This drum is not authentic nor is it an antiquity. I wouldn't even pay 1,000 Zimbabwean dollars or 1,000 Liberian dollars for it!"

What does Odakato know that Mineola doesn't? It is time to check facts.

Thesaurus

1. Write down two synonyms for *vendor*. _____ _____

2. Write one or two sentences explaining the difference between a vending machine and a vendor.

_____

_____

Image Search

Key Words: 🔍 *Plains Indians buffalo hide paintings*

1. Are there images of abstract and geometric designs? _____

2. Are there images of living things? _____

Atlas

Look at a U.S. state map. Which states make up the Four Corners region?

_____ _____ _____ _____

Search Engine/Encyclopedia

Write **True** or **False**. If your answer is **False**, cross out the incorrect word(s) and write the correct word(s) on the line.

_____ 1. Modern horses are native to the Americas. _____

_____ 2. Modern horses were first brought to the Americas by the English.

_____

Currency Converter

1. 1,000 Zimbabwean dollars (ZWD) = _____ U.S. dollars (USD)

2. 1,000 Liberian dollars (LRD) = _____ U.S. dollars (USD)

In Your Own Words

Could the drum be an authentic antiquity? On a separate piece of paper, write a paragraph in which you explain and support your reasoning.

Big River Man

"I know a swimmer who had piranhas eating his back," Jonathon said to Stephanie.

"Did this swimmer accidentally fall into the Amazon River?" asked Stephanie.

"The man was swimming in the Amazon, but it was no accident," Jonathon replied. "The swimmer's name is Martin Strel, who is known as 'Big River Man'. Strel is **tenacious**. He doesn't give up until he has swum the entire length of a river. Due to his tenacity, he swam the length of the Danube River, a distance of 1,780 miles. He swam the length of the Mississippi River, a distance of 3,885 kilometers. He also swam the 2,487-mile length of the Yangtze River."

"Then, in 2007, Strel swam the entire length of the Amazon River—a distance that is longer than the Atlantic Ocean is wide. Strel started in the headwaters of Peru and finished in the Brazilian city of Belem. It took him 66 days at an average 30,000 strokes per day to swim the 5,268 kilometers. Strel was attacked by piranhas a few times. Anyone less tenacious would have quit, but Strel found a clever way to deal with them."

"What did he do?" Stephanie asked.

"Oh, his support team kept a bucket of putrid blood in their boat. Whenever the piranhas attacked Strel, his helpers would quickly pour the bucket of blood into the water. The piranha would then all swim to the blood and leave Strel alone."

Jonathon continued, "Strel also suffered from severe sunburn. He ended up swimming in a big hat and a pillowcase over his face with slits cut out for his eyes. To try and prevent parasites from attacking, Strel wore a wetsuit coated with lanolin and Vaseline. Strel had to watch out for bull sharks, stingrays, anacondas, and huge logs. He even had to watch out for little piles of floating leaves because often there were wasps, stinging ants, and other poisonous insects resting on them. At one point, Strel's head buzzed for days from all the insect bites he had received."

"You know this is very hard to believe," Stephanie said.

"Oh, it's true all right," Jonathon said. "What's hard to believe is that Strel tenaciously stuck to his goal when he neared the coast. Tidal currents there were so strong that Strel was pushed backward despite swimming forward! Anyone less tenacious would have quit, but Strel swam at night to avoid the incoming tides. Do you know how dangerous that was? He couldn't see anything in the black water!"

"So Strel was young and foolish."

"What do you call young?" Jonathon asked. "Strel was 52 years old when he swam the Amazon. Who would think that when he was born in 1954 in Mokronog, Yugoslavia, he would achieve such a feat?"

"Aha!" exclaimed Stephanie. "I knew this was made up! There is no such place as Yugoslavia!"

Could Jonathon be making up the story about Strel? It is time to check facts.

Dictionary

1. What does *tenacious* mean? _____

2. Most likely, which proverb would a tenacious person follow?

    Ⓐ A bird in the hand is worth two in the bush.

    Ⓑ A rolling stone gathers no moss.

    Ⓒ No man is an island.

    Ⓓ If at first you don't succeed, try, try, again.

Metric Converter

Convert the measurements into miles or kilometers. In the last column, number the rivers from **1** to **4**, with **1** being the longest.

Danube	1,780 miles	_____ kilometers	_____
Mississippi	_____ miles	3,885 kilometers	_____
Yangtze	2,487 miles	_____ kilometers	_____
Amazon	_____ miles	5,268 kilometers	_____

Calculator

1. Strel swam a total distance of 5,268 km in 66 days. About how many kilometers per day is that?

    $5,268 \div 66 =$ _____

2. About how many miles per day is that?　**40**　**50**　**60**

Search Engine/Encyclopedia

1. What country and continent is Mokronog in? _____

2. Was Yugoslavia a country in 1954?　**Yes**　**No**

3. Did Strel swim the Amazon?　**Yes**　**No**

In Your Own Words

Were you surprised that Stephanie didn't believe Jonathon? On a separate piece of paper, use some of the facts from the story to explain your answer. At the end of your paragraph or in a short second paragraph, tell how you feel about Strel's swim. Could you be as tenacious? Would you want to be?

Fact Find #1: Nightingale Floors

Thesaurus

1. Possible answers include *odd*, *different*, and *strange*.
2. Possible answers include *typical*, *ordinary*, and *usual*.
3. turns it into its opposite (an antonym)

Image Search

1. Blarney
2. Blarney
3. No, it would be too heavy.

Search Engine/Encyclopedia

1. Tokyo
2. Dublin
3. The castles are not in the capital cities.

Fact Find #2: A Nose of Gold

Dictionary

1. helps you or is good for you
2. to raise money

Atlas

1. False, ~~Oslo~~, Copenhagen
2. True

Image Search: Yes

Temperature Converter

1. 1,981°F; much hotter
2. −434°F; much colder

Search Engine/Encyclopedia

1. Copper — Cu
2. Iron — Fe
3. Hydrogen — H
4. Gold — Au

Fact Find #3: The Lost City

Dictionary

1. human history, past cultures, and the way people lived
2. C

Image Search

1. cut out of rock, colorful, columns
2. narrow, tall, rocky sides

Atlas

1. Yes
2. Yes

Search Engine/Encyclopedia: right to left, top to bottom

Currency Exchange: Answers depend on the current exchange rate.

Fact Find #4: Visitor from Argentina

Thesaurus

1. huge, boundless, big, gigantic
2. Answers will vary.

Atlas

1. True
2. False, ~~Argentina~~, Brazil
3. False, ~~Pacific~~, Atlantic

Translator

1. I am so glad to be here today
2. giant anteater
3. anfibio = amphibian; mamífero = mammal; meant to say *mamífero*

Metric Converter

1. 39 to 47 inches
2. 27.5 or 28 to 35 inches
3. 23.6 or 24 inches

Image Search: Answers will vary.

Fact Find #5: The Alibi

Thesaurus

1. C

Image Search: beak should be longer than head

Temperature Converter

1. Yes

Calculator

1. B
2. C

Search Engine/Encyclopedia: Answers will vary, but the difference between the two times will be 16 or 17 hours.

Fact Find #6: Falling Faster than Sound

Dictionary

1. to fall or drop straight down at high speed

Calculator:

1. 19.47 miles
2. 229 mph

Image Search: Baumgartner's

Search Engine/ Encyclopedia

1. 768
2. No
3. "Yes" for all three.

Fact Find #7: RSVP

Thesaurus

1. Possible answers include *charmed*, *delighted*, and *captivated*.
2. Possible answers include *disgusted*, *repelled*, and *repulsed*.
3. Answers will vary.

Atlas

1. True
2. False, ~~Mediterranean Sea~~, English Channel.

Translator

1. "Respond, please" or "Respond, if you please"
2. Possible answers include *dear*, *honey*, and *sweetie*.
3. But why?
4. Non, merci.

Search Engine/Encyclopedia

1. 1401–1500
2. Central America
3. South America
4. North America

Paragraph corn, potatoes, and sunflowers would not have been introduced in Europe in 1422

Fact Find #8: The Highest Mountain

Thesaurus

1. Possible answers include *endurance* and *strength*.

Temperature Converter

1. -26°C, -73.3°C
2. 59°F, 24.8°F

Metric Converter

1. 8,848 m
2. 13,796 ft

Atlas

1. False, ~~Andes~~, Himalayan
2. False, ~~Bhutan~~, Tibet, China
3. False, ~~Oahu~~, Hawaii (also known as the Big Island)

Image Search: Mauna Kea

Fact Find #9: Grim, The Great White Shark

Dictionary

1. Possible answers include *irritate* and *annoy*.
2. C

Metric Converter

1. 9.2 ft
2. 112.7 km

Atlas

1. Yes
2. Yes
3. Yes

Search Engine/Encyclopedia

1. Yes
2. 1.15 miles, 1.85 km

Currency Converter: Answers depend on current rates.

Fact Find #10: Home to a Hospital and Blind Fish

Dictionary

1. Possible answers include *to rise and fall* and *to keep changing*.
2. D

Atlas: 7 (Missouri, Illinois, Indiana, Ohio, West Virginia, Virginia, Tennessee)

Image Search

1. No
2. Yes

Temperature Converter: A

Search Engine/Encyclopedia

1. False, ~~skin cancer~~, bacterial infection
2. False, ~~protects~~, does not protect
3. True

Fact Find #11: Long-Lost Relative

Dictionary

1. Possible answers include *a lie* and an *untrue statement*.
2. D

Calculator

1. $33.52
2. No

Search Engine/Encyclopedia

1. Prime Minister of England
2. Queen of England
3. day-month-year
4. Thames

Image Search
1. £
2. No

Fact Find #12: Where Pen Ink Freezes

Thesaurus
1. Possible answers include *freezing, chilly, ice-cold*

Atlas
1. Yes
2. No
3. No

Temperature Converter
1. -49°F
2. -61.6°F
3. -96.16°F

Translator:
1. (pronounced) "seevernyi olen"
2. (pronounced) "ha lowed nee"

Search Engine/Encyclopedia
1. Yes
2. caribou, polar bear

Fact Find #13: The Practical Ancient Wonder

Dictionary
1. Possible answers include *a very small amount* or *a bit.*
2. Yes, there is because it's all true.

Metric Converter
1. 459 feet
2. 183 meters
3. Yes

Image Search: Possible answers include *has a square bottom,* is *made up of three parts*, and *is not round.*

Encyclopedia/Search Engine
1. Yes
2. the Great Pyramid of Giza

Fact Find #14: Losing on Purpose

Thesaurus
1. B

Search Engine/Encyclopedia
1. False, ~~China~~, South Korea
2. False, ~~Edmonton~~, Ottawa
3. True
4. False, ~~St. Louis,~~ Jefferson City
5. Possible answers include gymnastics, volleyball, kayaking, judo, rowing, and boxing.

Calculator
1. 17.265–40.285
2. 27.78–64.82

Fact Find #15: Rare Animal Sightings

Dictionary: regularly found among particular people or in a certain area

Atlas
1. False, ~~Cancer~~, Capricorn
2. True
3. False, ~~Atlantic~~, Indian
4. True

Temperature Converter
1. 68.7°F to 76.5°F
2. 22°C to 27°C
3. Yes

Image Search
1. Tasmanian tiger
2. No

Search Engine/Encyclopedia
1. Yes
2. All are extinct.

Fact Find #16: Workers or Thieves?

Thesaurus
1. Possible answers include *strong, tough, enduring, fit, sound,* and *robust.*
2. A

Image Search
1. Yes
2. No

Metric Converter
1. 92.6 pounds
2. 38.8 pounds

Search Engine/Encyclopedia

1. Western United States
2. Yes
3. No

Fact Find #17: To Cross or Not Cross

Dictionary

1. Possible answers include *wordy*, *long-winded*, and *using more words than necessary*.
2. C

Metric Converter

1. 51.5km
2. 4392.5m

Image Search: Answers will vary depending on the image.

Atlas

1. Yes
2. Olympia

Search Engine/Encyclopedia

1. True
2. False, ~~Rocky Mountains~~, Cascade Range

Fact Find #18: Magellan's Diary

Thesaurus

1. Possible answers include *peaceful*, *quiet*, *calm*, and *tranquil*.
2. Possible answers include *hostile*, *violent*, *aggressive*, and *unfriendly*.
3. an open palm

Translator

1. Ferocious Sea
2. I do not speak the truth.

Atlas: B

Search Engine/Encyclopedia: Statements #3 and #5 are false. Only one ship and 18 men made it back. Magellan was killed in the Philippines.

Fact Find #19: Invasion from Mars

Dictionary

1. Possible answers include *difficult to understand* or *impossible to believe*.
2. Possible answers could be that germs were not capable of being measured back then, there were no microscopes, and people weren't educated about germs.

Search Engine/Encyclopedia

1. True
2. True
3. True
4. True
5. True

Atlas: Accept any answer between 50–65 miles.

Fact Find #20: Would You Hire this Person?

Dictionary

1. Possible answers include *of or relating to a star or stars* and *featuring the quality of a star or outstanding performer*.

Image Search

1. field of blue, white moon, and palm tree
2. field of blue, big dipper, and North Star

Search Engine/Encyclopedia

1. False, ~~eight~~, seven
2. False, ~~part~~, not part (or ~~Big Dipper,~~ Little Dipper)
3. True
4. True
5. False, ~~Major~~, Minor

Translator

1. dragon
2. major or greater bear
3. ram
4. crab
5. fish
6. scorpion
7. lion
8. swan

Fact Find #21: Elephant Dictionary

Thesaurus

1. Possible answers include *unlikely*, *far*, *detached*, and *isolated*.
2. C

Calculator

1. 7,300 miles
2. about 2.7 miles

Images: The place has clear views, one can know that elephants will go there, etc.

Atlas

1. West
2. North
3. No

Search Engine/Encyclopedia

1. Salem
2. Yes
3. Yes

Fact Find #22: Central America Map

Thesaurus

1. Possible answers include *hasty*, *thoughtless*, *reckless*, and *imprudent*.

Metric Converter

1. 50.95
2. No

Calculator

1. 2.7
2. 40.27
3. No

Search Engine/Encyclopedia

1. C
2. Guatemala, Belize, El Salvador, Honduras, Nicaragua, Costa Rica, Panama

Fact Find #23: A Perfect Arrangement

Dictionary

1. has a distinctive and typically pleasant smell
2. A

Atlas: All should be checked.

Temperature Converter: 71.6°F (or 72°F)

Search Engine/Encyclopedia

1. huge, heavy, parasitic, smells like rotting flesh
2. poison ivy or oak, lacquer tree
3. thorn-covered, can smell like dirty socks or rotten onions

Translator: You smell as good as these flowers!

Fact Find #24: Buffalo Drum

Thesaurus

1. Possible answers include *merchant, peddler, salesperson*, and *seller*.
2. vendor is a person selling, not a machine

Image Search

1. Yes
2. Yes

Atlas: Colorado, New Mexico, Arizona, Utah

Search Engine/Encyclopedia

1. False, ~~native~~, not native
2. False, ~~English~~, Spanish

Currency Converter: Answers will depend on the current exchange rate, but they will most likely be very low.

Fact Find #25: Big River Man

Dictionary

1. Possible answers include *holding fast, persistent*, and *not giving up*.
2. D

Metric Converter: Danube = 2,865 km (4th); Mississippi = 2,414 miles (3rd); Yangtze = 4,002 km (2nd); Amazon = 3,273 miles (1st)

Calculator:

1. 79.8 km (or 80 km)
2. 50

Search Engine/Encyclopedia

1. Slovenia, Europe
2. Yes
3. Yes